Where Whirlwinds Took Them:
Journeys of Two New Mexico Families

I0104606

Moises Sandoval

Publisher:

Moises Sandoval Communications
West Hartford, CT 06107
E-mail: moises473@comcast.net

Queries regarding rights and permissions should be addressed to Moises Sandoval Communications, 473 Fern, W. Hartford, CT 06107.

Sandoval, Moises.
Where Whirlwinds Took Them: Journeys of Two New Mexico Families.

ISBN-978-0-578-05020-1 (pbk)

TABLE OF CONTENTS

FOREWORD

Although not from New Mexico, I, in many ways, identify with New Mexico. Born and raised in El Paso, I have never felt an affinity with the rest of Texas. When I moved to California some forty years ago, some there would ask me if I was a "Tejano."

"No," I would respond, "we never used that term in El Paso that is more widely an expression of Mexican American identity in other parts of Texas especially in the southern portions."

I remember as a young high school student at Cathedral High School in El Paso travelling to Santa Fe to play football against St. Michael's High and identifying with the landscape as our bus followed the classic El Camino Real from El Paso to Santa Fe. The City of Santa Fe with its historic Hispano culture made for a familiar fit.

In more recent years, I have had more opportunities to revisit New Mexico, in particular Santa Fe and Albuquerque as my wife, Professor Ellen McCracken, and I began a biography of Fray Angélico Chávez, the renowned New Mexican Franciscan historian, writer, and artist. Beginning in the mid-1990s we went to New Mexico every summer to research our project and to do numerous interviews with people who could share their memories of Fray Angélico. Through these many visits and encounters with New Mexicans including many Hispanos, I increased my connection with the "Land of Enchantment" and its peoples and in particular its deeply-rooted Hispano history, culture, and traditions.

It is this strong affair with Hispanic New Mexico that draws me to the wonderful family oral history that Moises Sandoval has written and produced. Through these wide-ranging stories, we get a sense and understanding not only of Sandoval's extended family based out of Terromote, but of the Hispano experience in New Mexico. Using a generational approach, Sandoval presents a broad panorama of historical continuity and change among Hispanos.

Through the history recounted of the elders—the Grandparents Generation—we learn about those who in many ways represented what I call the Conquered Generation in Mexican American or Chicano history. This is that generation that inherited from their own parents the legacy of the U.S. conquest of New Mexico in the mid-1840s and the ethnic, racial, and cultural changes, among others, that came in its wake. One of the challenges of the conquest was the efforts of incoming

Anglo Americans or Euro-Americans to re-possess the sacred lands held by the Hispanos. Through a variety of means a good deal of land transfers occurred and yet the story does not stop here.

Many, like those in Sandoval's family, struggled to hold on to their lands in Terromote and elsewhere not just for material reasons but for cultural ones as well. The land–*la tierra*–represented family, culture, and identity. Because of their historical agency to hold on to their lands despite many obstacles, Sandoval's ancestors helped to maintain a crucial land base for the preservation of Hispano culture.

Yet continuity expressed through the land also came with change. The descendants of the elders facing increased economic pressures such as during the Great Depression were forced to leave their lands and become permanent or temporary migrant workers and relocated to other areas such as Colorado to pick crops or to find other work to sustain their families and their lands left behind.

Many of these oral histories, especially of Moises Sandoval's own generation, reflect such changes. In addition, access to more education than their parents as well as the geographic mobility ushered in by World War II and the many Hispano G.I.'s who went off to "The Good War," all produced cultural and material changes that added to the acculturation of this generation.

Yet, as Sandoval's oral histories reveal, many of these more mobile Hispanos still retained a connection to their ancestral lands. There was something in their genes or their *"cultura"* that drew them back in one form or another.

The same is true for the newer generations, the children of Moises Sandoval and others. Despite their even greater mobility and success, many retain or rediscover this marvelous affinity for the lands of their parents and grandparents. Continuity and change–this characterizes the stories contained in this valuable and highly readable volume.

As a practitioner of many oral history projects, I very much appreciate Moises Sandoval's contributions in chronicling his family history through the medium of oral history. This valuable historical tool and perspective does what no other historical method does: it brings to life the history of ordinary men and women who as these stories reveal are not so ordinary, but in fact exceptional individuals tied together by strong family ties. This does not mean that there are no family tragedies in these relationships. All families have conflicts and family secrets and these stories attest to this.

But, at the same time, we also find resilient and determined people who overcome various forms of direct and indirect discrimination and personal crises to survive and more than survive to achieve their hard-fought place in the history of New Mexico and the United States. Sandoval's history is both a New Mexico story and a human story and readers from all backgrounds will find themselves in these narratives.

I want to conclude this Foreword by thanking Moises Sandoval for asking me to write it. This is a great honor coming from a man whose work and career I very much admire. Moises Sandoval is a ground-breaking journalist whose extensive writings and editing of such journals as *Maryknoll Magazine* and *Revista Maryknoll* are exemplary. Sandoval is a pioneer in Latino Catholic history and in Latino Catholic journalism. I know of no other journalist of Latino background with the remarkable and productive record that Moises Sandoval has accomplished. His achievements and own personal success and mobility are inspirational and remarkable.

And yet, like those in his family oral history, he has never forgotten who he is and where he came from. He has never strayed too far from his ancestral lands because it is this sense of place that anchors his identity. By bringing to light this family history, Moises Sandoval further comes home.

Mario T. García
Professor of Chicano Studies and History
University of California, Santa Barbara.

DEDICATION

To my mother, Amada Perea Sandoval, my inspiration then and even now when she is no longer here. She lived half a century in Brighton, CO, and felt more and more at home with each passing decade. Her father was buried there, as were her husband and three sons. But in her heart of hearts she knew it was still a Diaspora, for her last words on the day she died were: "I am going to New Mexico today."

ACKNOWLEDGMENTS

I am grateful, first of all, to all those who contributed their oral histories and memoirs or who shared the information for their profiles. José A. Perea shared not only his own story but also essential details of Grandfather Enrique Perea's life and of other members of the family. Lucy Sandoval Branch provided not only her own memoir of growing up in Brighton but also interviewed Aunt Dulcinea Olivas and sent me many of the photos used in this book. Richard Perea shared his own research on the family, photos he has gathered over the years and read the final manuscript. My daughter Meg, experienced in book production, proofread and corrected the layouts.

I am also grateful to Dr. Santos Vega for providing valuable organizational and editing counsel and for showing me the way to publish this work so that those up in age, as the author himself, will be able to see it in print and to rejoice in the long and fruitful journey of their families. In a special way, I want to thank Professor Mario Garcia for doing the Foreword and for his advice and encouragement. Long before I met him a few years ago, I admired his work as a historian.

Tim Matovina, director of the Cushwa Center for the Study of American Catholicism at Notre Dame University, read an early draft of the manuscript and made helpful suggestions, as did my long-time friend, Father Juan Romero, a paisano from Taos and Los Angeles.

In large measure this book was also made possible by an Alicia Patterson Foundation grant I received in 1977 to study the Hispanic people of the United States. It was the only sabbatical I had in more than a half-century in journalism. In the course of my travels to fulfill the requirements of the grant, I interviewed members of my family about their history.

Finally, since this book is about the homeland we carry with us, I could not have spent the hours, days, years and decades I have worked on these memories without the homeland provided by my wife, Penny, and our children: Meg, Michael, Rose, Jim, and Mary.

THE LONGEST JOURNEY

Human DNA originated about 275,000 years ago with a man born in Eastern Africa. For the Sandoval family, its female DNA goes back 150,000 to 200,000 years in the same region.

Over many thousands of years the first humans populated Africa, the Mediterranean region, Europe, Asia and other then known continents in the Old World. The family of lineages that contained my father's DNA, classified R1, originated in Central Asia between the Caspian steppes and the Hindu Kush 20,000 to 34,000 years ago.

The DNA of my mother goes back at least 30,000 years to Eurasia. Now classified as Haplogroup A, it was brought to the Americas by people now known as Native Americans. They crossed from Asia to Alaska via a land bridge where the Bering strait is now. Over millennia they populated North and South America, the last two continents to be settled by humans.

My father's DNA migrated westward to the Middle East, lands now in Ukraine, the Mediterranean, the Iberian Peninsula, now Spain and Portugal, and finally to the Americas. Along the way the DNA underwent several mutations and is now classified as R1b1b2. But some Sandovals also have the DNA of European Jews, classified as J2.

In my mother's family, her ancestors, besides the Native Americans, were Semites. The male DNA of the Pereas, classified as J1, originated in the Middle East about 10,000 years ago. It spread throughout the Middle East, the Mediterranean and North Africa. Sephardic Jews and Arab Moors belong to this family of lineages. Today, on the east side of the Jordan River in Palestine, there is a place named Perea.

My DNA therefore shows I am 49 percent European: 17% Iberian, 12% Irish, 12% Italian and Greek, and 2% of each of the following ethnicities, British, European Jewish, Scandinavian and Eastern European; 35% Native American, 7% North African, 5% Central Asian, and 4% Middle Eastern, including Armenian and Syrian-Lebanese. I also have traces of Polynesian and Filipino DNA.

With such variety of DNA, I could call almost any region of the planet home and every inhabitant my brother or sister, or at least my cousin. Indeed, all animosities aside, we are all related. There are no aliens among us.

INTRODUCTION

"In many ways I didn't know where I came from. So I was drawn to the belief that you could sustain a spiritual, emotional and cultural identity. And I understand the Zionist idea–that there is always a homeland at the center of our identity."

President Barack Obama, in a talk to American Jews on June 4, 2008

This book is about two families entering a new stage in a long history of migration. They were leaving a remote and isolated rural homeland in northern New Mexico, some moving to nearby cities but most moving to a larger, more challenging, and at times, hostile world. Centuries before then, the Pereas and the Sandovals had left their homeland in the Basque region and the provinces of Extremadura and Andalucía in Spain, respectively, to move to the new world. In stages, they had migrated to the Caribbean, Mexico and, finally, New Mexico. Each time they moved within the mantle of Spanish culture and hegemony. This time most of them were moving to an Anglo culture that generally did not welcome them, especially those who moved to other states. The oral histories, memoirs and profiles in this book describe what happened to them.

They faced formidable obstacles as they began. They were poor because their farms were small and produced only for subsistence. They spoke little or no English because they lived in isolated communities where only Spanish was spoken. Their schools went only to the eighth grade and few students graduated. They were almost completely removed from the modern world. Their homes had no electricity and their farms no motorized implements or vehicles. Water had to be drawn manually from hand-dug wells. They had pit privies instead of modern plumbing. At their destinations, they were considered fit only for common labor–picking vegetables, thinning, hoeing or harvesting beets, working as railroad track laborers or shepherds.

They also had a few assets. They knew how to survive in the harsh high desert of the foothills of the Sangre de Cristo Mountains. They knew how to save some of the little money they made. They could build with stone, logs and adobe–skills now forgotten. They had united families and communities; there were few if any divorces. They had a deep faith they practiced faithfully. They could defer the gratification of hearth and family to go work for months or years in Wyoming and other neighboring states, sending most of their money home to their families.

Several decades back I visited sociologist Ellwyn R. Stoddard at the University of Texas in El Paso. He had written an important book about Mexican Americans. As I regaled him about how poor we had been, he exclaimed: "Your family had middle class values." As I began to look into the history not only of my immediate family but also of the extended family and its vast network of relationships in the area, I saw that they had done the same things other groups had done: work hard, make sacrifices, learn wherever they found themselves, build strong families, and practice their faith. These are behaviors of middle class society.

These New Mexicans were not confined in common labor for long. My family moved to Brighton, CO, in 1944 where we worked in the fields alongside about 50 other families. In the 1970s I went back to find out how many of those families were still picking peas and beans; only two remained. Despite fierce discrimination, they soon found jobs in meat packing houses, bakeries, construction and other industries. They bought their own homes, settling in integrated neighborhoods instead of creating their own ghettoes. Their sons and daughters went to high school and graduated, some with honors. Soon some were going to college and earning degrees. The great grandchildren of the Pereas and Sandovals went to Yale and Harvard and other prestigious universities. Among them, one finds medical doctors, a lawyer, a publisher, a pharmacist, people in religious life, missionaries, journalists, teachers and college professors. Others founded their own businesses, among them restaurants, landscape contracting, construction, auto repair shops, and gas stations. They integrated into the larger society but retained their own culture. Clearly these people who began with so little achieved success by any measure. (See the directory on page 157.)

They advanced at a time when they had no models within their own families, no one who had graduated from high school, much less college. In New Mexico, Hispanics have always had some leaders who educated themselves, won elected office or had businesses. But that was not true in other states to where they moved. In Colorado, we knew of no Hispanic who had become a lawyer, doctor, professor or teacher, priest, businessman or even electrician, plumber or carpenter. At one time, it was more difficult to become an apprentice in a trade union than to get into college. Moreover, these families succeeded when the predominant view in the mainstream culture was that they were incapable. Consequently, they were often denied the opportunity for better jobs and higher education.

One of the purposes of this book is to show how they did it, what values enabled them to get ahead, how they had to sacrifice, how they evolved big dreams from the elemental drive to survive. Another is to show that Hispanics can succeed as any other group in America, for unfortunately many in the larger society see their culture as one of failure. In 1997 the Mexican American Legal Defense and Educational Fund (MALDEF) ran a 30-second commercial showing scenes from Latino life: parents with children, buying a home, teachers in classrooms, soldiers returning from war, and graduation. But non-Hispanic whites who participated in focus group discussions of the commercial ultimately found it unbelievable, seeing Latinos as a culture of failure, unable to get ahead despite having a good work ethic, unable to do anything other than menial labor.[1]

More than just about the Pereas and Sandovals, this book is about their vast extended families surnamed Vigil, Aragon, Cordoba, Romero, Padilla, Jimenez, Trujillo, Lucero, Suazo, Abeyta, Aragon, Montoya, Quintana, Gomez and Duran. All are in Fray Angélico Chávez's classic book on the first families in New Mexico.[2] They lived in foothill communities beginning a dozen miles north of Las Vegas–Sapello, San Ignacio, Manuelitas, Terromote, Peñasco, La Cebolla, Rociada and Gascon. I call them the people of Terromote, a local word meaning whirlwind, because it is more evocative of the destiny that overtook them all. They were scattered all over the country by a migration largely unnoticed by historians.

In 1847 when the United States seized the Southwest from Mexico, including lands now the states of Texas, New Mexico, Arizona, California, Nevada and parts of Colorado and Oklahoma, much was written about the Americans and European immigrants who moved into the new territories. What little was written about Hispanics focused only on their retreat or expulsion into Mexico. Particularly in Texas and California, where Hispanics then numbered only 5,000 and 8,000, respectively, they were quickly overwhelmed. Thus it was felt, according to the historian Carey McWilliams, that the Hispanic, like the Indian, was destined to disappear.

But it was different in New Mexico, home of 60,000 of the 75,000 Hispanics who became U.S. citizens with the signing of the treaty of Guadalupe Hidalgo in 1848. Migration to Mexico occurred only along the border. They remained the majority of the population for three quarters of a century, the reason why statehood was delayed until 1912. But many rural areas remained almost exclusively Hispanic for much longer, as in the communities where my family originated. It is in New Mexico that historian Carey McWilliams' observation best applied: "…they are still as firmly rooted in the Southwest as a forest of Joshua trees….The Spanish-speaking have an identification with the Southwest which can never be broken. They are not interlopers or immigrants but an indigenous people."[3] These people did not come to the United States; it came to them and that made all the difference. Rather than fleeing south, they were soon moving north east and west in search of opportunity.

That trend started with the opening of the Santa Fe Trail in 1821, linking St. Louis and Santa Fe. During the 60 years that traders traveled the 800-mile route, New Mexicans were often the drivers of the mules and oxen pulling the wagons. The Pereas, my mother´s family, were proprietors of Perea Mercantile in Bernalillo, NM. They ran wagon trains to Mexico City, St. Louis, and San Francisco. When the Mormons settled in Utah in 1847, they drove herds of sheep and wagon trains of supplies to them.[4] The contacts made during those journeys led Rumaldo Perea, one of my great grandfather´s sons, to move his family of 15 children to Columbia, Utah (in Carbon County), in 1917. A blacksmith, he made tools for the coal mines as well as for carpentry. He also made caskets for the local mortician.[5] Today the telephone directory´s white pages in Utah contain 129 unique Perea names, undoubtedly most of them from the clan Rumaldo established.

Archives at Notre Dame University list Pereas from Bernalillo among its students in the mid-1800s.[6] Later in the 19th century, two attended a Jesuit academy in St. Louis and one attended a military academy in New York.

In my father´s family, Agustin Sandoval, half-brother of my grandfather Octaviano Sandoval, moved to Colorado in the late 19th century and became a wealthy highway contractor, according to my father, Eusebio. At some point, my grandfather Octaviano also worked in

Wyoming as a shepherd. At first, the men left their families to work for a season, months or sometimes years, returning home to buy land or livestock. These sojourns increased as time went by. But eventually they moved permanently, driven by hard times, especially during the Great Depression, or lured by the work opportunities that opened up during World War II. The first moves were usually to neighboring states—Colorado, Wyoming, Utah, Arizona, California, Oklahoma and Texas—then beyond. My father's turn came in the 1920s, when he started going to Wyoming to work as a track laborer for the Union Pacific or as a shepherd. In 1944, he got a job in a meat packing house in Denver and, after a few months, moved our family to Brighton, CO. Our extended family now lives all over the country, even in Alaska.

This book is also about our homeland, for I believe it made our migration possible and insured its success. With a 300-year history in New Mexico by the turn of the 20th century, we Hispanics had roots that could not be eradicated. Our markers were everywhere, in the names of rivers, towns and counties; the irrigation systems; the chapels and churches, building crafts, art and traditions. To borrow President Obama's words, we had a "spiritual, emotional and cultural identity," with an unbreakable bond between past and present. We were so secure in our homeland that we could leave it with the confidence that it could not be taken away and that we could always return. Moreover, when the Pereas and Sandovals left their rural communities they took part of their homeland with them. All immigrants bring that complex of values, worldview and way of being with them. If worthy, the homeland we carry within us almost foreordains our success.

What we achieve is the product not only of our own efforts but of the achievements of those who come before us, somehow not just the ancestors we knew but also remote ones as well. Though we may know little about their lives, what they yearned and worked for seems to be imprinted in our DNA. The Sandovals, more rural than urban, had (and still have) great reverence for the land. The Pereas, more urban, were (and are) more likely to be in business and public life. In the long history of the Pereas and the Sandovals there is much to inspire present and future generations of these families.

Although it is not known when the Pereas came to the Americas, they apparently already lived in the El Paso area when the Indians revolted in 1680 and expelled the Spaniards from New Mexico. Fray Angélico Chávez wrote that in 1681 Juan de Perea, 50 years old and unmarried (perhaps a widower) joined Otermin's troops at Guadalupe del Paso, where Juan de Perea, then 18 and single, passed muster with his mother and brethren the same year. In 1693, the younger Perea and his wife, Aldonsa, came to Santa Fe with colonists following the reconquest of the territory by Diego de Vargas. He was described as a soldier, "a native of New Mexico." Another couple, Esteban de Perea and his wife, Francisca Garcia, appear at the same time, although Chávez could not ascertain whether they came with the reconquest or were already in New Mexico. Research by Cousin Richard Perea traces the Perea family for 11 generations to those first settlers. In Madrid, Spain, where Cousin Chris Suazo directs the department of instrumental music at the American School, he traced the Perea family to that country's Basque region.

The Pereas appear frequently in New Mexico's history. Francisco Perea, whose maternal grandfather was governor at the beginning of the Mexican period (1821-1846), served in the territorial legislature in the 1850s, then as a lieutenant colonel in the Union forces during the Civil War, participating in the Union victory at Apache Canyon, and between 1863 and 1865 was the territory's delegate to Congress. During his sojourn in Washington, he became a friend of Abraham Lincoln and was sitting near him in the Ford theatre the night the President was assassinated. He was a cousin of my great grandfather.

My great grandparents, Juan Perea and Quirina Romero, came from Albuquerque. They settled in Los Martinez, near Manuelitas. A blacksmith skilled at repairing wagons, he would go on expeditions to hunt buffalo and came back with a lot of dried meat.[7] They had five sons and three daughters, Enrique, my grandfather; Rumaldo, the Utah pioneer; Encarnación, Alejandro, Adolfo, Alcarita, Albinita and Juanita. For a time Enrique managed a big ranch in San Ignacio and taught in a one-room school in the community of Los Aguajes, then farmed 200 acres he bought in 1917 near Terromote. Encarnación had a farm of several hundred acres in Manuelitas, now owned by his daughter, Agustina, a single woman 88 years old in 2009. Alejandro lived and worked in the Las Vegas area and Adolfo had a grocery store in Rowe, a village near Pecos.

The Sandovals, from the provinces of Andalucía and Extremadura in Southern Spain, came to the New World in earliest Spanish voyages. Gonzalo de Sandoval, born in Medellin, sailed from Spain in mid-November 1516 and was living in Cuba when Hernan Cortés, also from

Medellin, recruited him for the expedition to conquer Mexico. Though then only 22, Sandoval served as a captain, second in command to the 34-year-old Cortés. Bernal Diaz del Castillo, the chronicler of the conquest (*La Verdadera Historia de La Conquista de La Nueva España*)[8] described Sandoval as a brave and successful commander with qualities somewhat uncommon among the conquistadores–lack of avarice, compassion for the conquered and unswerving loyalty to Cortés. He received one of 20 Indian maidens given to Cortés by the cacique of Tabasco early in the conquest, but history left no record of children from that union. Sandoval, however, returned to Spain alone and died there at the age of 31. Clinton H. Gardiner, his biographer, wrote that before leaving Mexico he willed all his possessions in the New World to a cousin, Juan de Sandoval. More likely, the Sandovals of the New World descended from him or from Pedro de Sandoval, also in the

Great grandparents Quirina and Juan Perea.

Cortés expedition.[9] But history left no record.

The Sandovals next appear in 1693, when, according to Fray Chávez, Juan de Dios Sandoval, his wife, Juana, and their 18-year-old son Miguel arrived in New Mexico following the reconquest. Juan was the son of Jacinto de Sandoval and Juana de Estrada, natives of Mexico City. In 1714 Miguel was a captain in the Spanish garrison in New Mexico. He and his wife, Lucia Gomez, had eight children, of whom one of their four sons, Andres, Antonio, Juan Manuel or Felipe is our ancestor.

As they spread to many parts of New Mexico, the Sandovals were prominent in military service, ranching, politics and government. Sandoval County, north of Albuquerque, was named for the first settler, Juan de Dios Sandoval. The town of Sandoval, in the same county, was named for a leading cattleman.

My great grandfather Estanislado Sandoval was born in Manuelitas in 1821, four miles downstream from Terromote. As a young man, according to family lore, he was abducted by plains Indians. After a short time he escaped with the help of an Indian young woman who one night provided him with a horse and a rawhide bag filled with balls of blue cornmeal mush. He rode all night and then abandoned the horse to make it easier to hide. He hid in arroyos during daylight and walked at night, finding his way home after several narrow escapes.

Estanislado married Loreta Garcia and, according to baptismal records from Our Lady of Guadalupe in Sapello, now in the archdiocesan archives in Santa Fe, they had three children: Agustin, born in 1862; Maria Santos del Refugio, born in 1864, and Ramona, born in 1865. After his wife died Estanislado apparently lived with but never married an Indian woman named Ricarda Jimenez. They had two children, Octaviano and Luisa, born in 1874 and 1875, respectively, according to the 1880 census.

Great grandfather Estanislado had a piece of land near Terromote, probably part of the Las Vegas land grant. His son Octaviano inherited it and acquired several hundred acres more in exchange for a horse and saddle he bought with money saved while working as a shepherd in Wyoming. Most of this land remains in Sandoval hands, including those of the author and his siblings.

The oral histories, memoirs or profiles are categorized in chapters dealing with the homeland, the grandparents, sons and daughters, the school that gave them a quantum leap into the future, memories of the grandchildren, the move to Las Vegas, Brighton and beyond, work challenges, the fight against discrimination, triumphs and tragedies, religion's influence, military service, Brighton's deep imprint, the roots of success and an epilogue.

---

[1]David E. Hayes-Bautista, *La Nueva California: Latinos in the Golden State* (Berkeley: University of California Press, 2004) Introduction.
[2]Fray Angélico Chávez, *Origins of New Mexico Families: A Genealogy of the Spanish Colonial Period* (Santa Fe: Museum of New Mexico Press, 1992).
[3]Carey McWilliams, *North from Mexico: The Spanish-Speaking People of the United States* (New York: Greenwood Press, 1968), p. 9.
[4]Research by Richard Perea.
[5]E-mail from Perry Perea, a grandson. He is a dentist living in St. Louis, MO.
6Research by Richard Perea.
[7]Amada Sandoval, interview with Moises Sandoval, 1977.
[8]Bernal Diaz del Castillo, *La Verdadera Historia de La Conquista de La Nueva España* (Porrúa, México: 1960) Vol: II, p. 352.
[9]Clinton H. Gardiner, *The Constant Captain: Gonzalo de Sandoval* (Carbondale, IL: Southern Illinois University Press, 1961) p. vii.

A Place Named Whirlwind

In my walks in the foothills of the Sangre de Cristo Mountains, my homeland, I often look into the long-abandoned farmhouses, small buildings of stone or logs, plastered outside with the red-clay soil common here and inside whitewashed with calcimine. I see these as the birthplace of dreams fulfilled elsewhere. I see these artifacts not a symbol of a way of life that has disappeared, as strangers often see them, but as a way of life still alive and relevant in the modern world in places we never imagined when we were growing up here.

At the ruins of Grandfather Octaviano Sandoval's stone house, I see broken homemade tables, crude cupboards made with hand-tools, and the springs of an abandoned bed. The collapsing roof creaks as the persistent wind, perhaps the most common feature of these highlands, rips it apart one tin panel at a time. Here and there the rough-hewn or peeled pine beams have collapsed and rain and snow have rotted the pine-plank floor. Everything of any value was taken long ago but a religious calendar still hangs on a nail on one wall, with a color photo of Our Lady of Guadalupe, one clue to the culture of those who lived there.

Ruins of Grandfather Octaviano's house.

The frame of a Model-T Ford, wheels and engine gone, and the skeleton of a black wood stove rust in the yard. Here and there lie rusted links and buckles once part of leather harnesses for horses. The metalwork was obviously pounded into shape in a crude forge. Rain and snow have eroded away the adobe plaster from the top of a stone horno, an outdoor oven shaped like a giant wasp's nest where my grandmother once baked bread and roasted corn on the cob. Nearby lie the ruins of the house where I was born, its roof caved in, the door and window frames fallen out and walls steadily going down, stone by stone. No one has lived here for half a century.

About a mile away stands the house of my Uncle Filadelfio Aragon. He moved to Brighton, CO, in 1942 only to die crushed by a train rail that slipped off a crane in 1948. A can of green beans, perhaps left by a passing hippie decades ago, sits in the simple cupboard. Soil drifted by the wind has partially buried a plow and a harrow in the yard.

The place is Terromote, located in the eastern foothills of the Sangre de Cristo Mountains in New Mexico. But, today, if you tell people you are from Terromote, even if they live only 20 or 30 miles away, they give you a blank look. You can't find it on any road sign or map. In 1965 when a new geological survey was made of the area, the mapmakers did not find the word Terromote in any classical Spanish dictionary. Perhaps assuming the inhabitants simply did not know how to spell the name of their own homeland, they renamed it Tierra Monte, meaning forest land. Even Cousin Josephine Jacquez, who spent part of her youth in Terromote, saw the name as a symbol of the backwardness of the people. "Grandpa's farm was in Tierra Monte, but people got careless and called it Terromote," she wrote in a brief autobiography. Terromote, however, is an authentic word, found in *A Dictionary of New Mexico and Southern Colorado Spanish*, by Ruben Cobos, and meaning whirlwind.

Tierra Monte, though not at all what the original describes, is apt enough, since undulating waves of Ponderosa forest leap westward across a vast landscape to peaks rising almost to 11,000 feet above sea level. Dominating the vista is an unusual mountain with a silhouette like a covered wagon. It was named Hermit's Peak, for an eccentric Catholic religious Brother, Juan Maria Agostini, an Italian penitent, who lived on the mountain from 1863-1867, carving crucifixes and religious emblems he traded for food. Like the people of Terromote, the whirlwind took him too—to a mountain in southern New Mexico where he died a violent death at the hands of unknown assailants.

Terromote, rather than Tierra Monte, is more indicative of the character of the land and the fate of its people. These uplands are prone to sudden violent whirlwinds that lift spirals of red soil off tilled fields, lift the roofs off houses or knock over a stand of trees. Similarly, as if caught in the power of the whirlwind, the people who once lived in Terromote scattered to the four winds, from Alaska to San Diego, Miami to Washington, D.C., New York to San Francisco and many places in between.

But rather than simply settling into the anonymity of urban life, they brought whirlwinds of their own, some gentle, some fierce, gaining notoriety, sometimes fame. They challenged the status quo, refusing to accept "their place," and if not always winning, always striving and making a difference. They refused to be segregated in the barrios, in public accommodations, regions of the country and even in their choice of spouses, often marrying outside their own group. They fought the notion that they were suited only for common labor.

Hermit's Peak as it appears from the Sandoval ranch in Terromote.

How could an isolated land and a culture seen as poor and backward prepare us so well to make our way in the modern world? It would be difficult to find a place more anonymous and out of the way, yet so close to Santa Fe, the capital, roughly 80 miles by road but only about half that distance in a straight line over the Sangre de Cristo peaks of the Pecos wilderness. To get to Terromote from Santa Fe, one takes I-25 north, which actually goes south, then east, northeast and finally north to Las Vegas, once a notorious frontier town along the Santa Fe Trail and later along the railroad, a haven for outlaws, drovers and cowboys, but now a quiet town of 14,020 with a median family income of $24,000. The largest employers are the state mental hospital, New Mexico Highlands University, Luna Community College and Wal-Mart, the closest thing to a shopping center. Until I was 14 Las Vegas was the only city I knew, full of wonders like electric lights.

The drive from Las Vegas to Terromote takes half an hour today. But in the twenties and thirties it took eight hours by horse-drawn wagon or buggy, the only vehicles that most of the farmers of Terromote had. You take state Highway 518 north on Seventh Street, past the Wal-Mart and a drive-in theatre. Three miles out, the road skirts Storrie Lake, a man-made dam providing water for the meadows that fringe the road (Las Vegas means the meadows in Spanish). From there the road goes through a wide expanse of mostly flat grassland here and there with sparse junipers and small stands of scrub oak. To the west lie the foothills of the Sangre de Cristo Mountains, to the east the endless emptiness of the plains.

After 12 miles, at the confluence of two little mountain streams fringed with cottonwoods, willows, orchards and meadows, 518 comes to Sapello–a scattering of houses, a post office, a Chevron service station with a convenience store and the chapel of Our Lady of Guadalupe. Until 1957, Our Lady of Guadalupe was a parish. Its book of baptisms had the only official record of my birth. In those days, everyone was born at home with the help of midwives and they did not report births to the county or state.

At Sapello, 518 finally enters a valley leading north to the village of Mora 18 miles away. State Highway 94, the road to Terromote, begins there, with a left turn by the Chevron station. Now paved, 94 was a dirt road when I was a boy, its red clay a quagmire after summer rains or winter snows. The road climbs up a long hill to the northwest and, at the top, Highway 266 branches to the left, leading to San Ignacio, six miles away. Highway 94 branches to the right, with two road signs, one for Manuelitas, several miles up the road, and Pendaries, a vacation community about 12 miles away. Manuelitas lies in a broad valley fed by a small mountain stream flowing from the Pecos wilderness. Meadows, cottonwoods, lush gardens, orchards of plum and apple trees mark the course of the river. Nowhere along Highway 94–now or in the past–has there been a road sign for Terromote.

Continuing steadily uphill beyond Manuelitas, 94 goes past the chapel of San Ysidro, in whose cemetery many of my ancestors are buried. Here the landscape changes from green to grey. Junipers and piñons give way to Ponderosa pines. There are no rivers here; deep arroyos scar the bottom of the narrow valleys. Terromote begins here, about two miles beyond the chapel, with small farms along Highway 94 and hidden in the valleys on both sides. But the only landmark that once identified it, a one-room stone building called Terromote School, is now just a pile of stones. Terromote ends four miles farther at Peñasco where the road drops steeply into the Cebolla Valley, on maps sometimes identified as Quebraditas Valley. There state Highway 103 branches to the left en route to Rociada and Pendaries Village and 94 turns eastward toward Le Doux and Mora, ending in the center of the village at its intersection with 518, its total length no more than 20 miles.

Terromote is the driest land along Highway 94. It is what is called high desert, 7,500 feet above sea level, prone to drought that cracks the soil like the floor of a dry lake, shrivels the crops and dries the grass needed by livestock. At such times when I was a boy, the farmers, singing hymns and chanting prayers for rain, walked in procession through the fields carrying the statue of San Ysidro, the patron saint of farmers. Even in wet years, the land yielded only for subsistence, never for cash income. The men therefore often left their families to work for months and sometimes years as track laborers or shepherds in Wyoming and Utah or in the mines in Pecos.

At that time, the farmers had no electricity, tractors or motor vehicles. Horses pulled the plows, harrows and wagons. Two-man crosscut saws cut the timber to sell as mine props and railroad ties or build log cabins or barns. Women washed clothing on a washboard in a tub. Water was drawn by the bucket from hand-dug wells. Meat, fruits and vegetables had to be canned or dried for the winter, the only way to preserve them. Homes, barns and other farm buildings were built with hand tools. Since the parish priest in Sapello rarely came to celebrate Mass in San Ysidro, the Penitentes and their sister organization, the Carmelitas, presided over our religious services. When someone became sick, the people relied on home remedies, almost never able to see a doctor in Las Vegas.

The hard, unforgiving land and the harsh living conditions therefore shaped the character of the people, forcing them to work hard, develop strong religious and family values, to sacrifice for survival and for the future.

Scenes from the Homeland

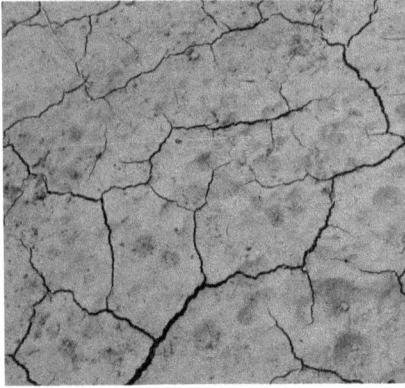

Left, the cracked earth when it is dry; right, abundant water in those years when the rains are plentiful.

The ruins of Filadelfio Aragon's home, abandoned 70 years ago.

A profusion of flowers during the good years.

Winter wonderland leading to the author's home on Sandoval ranch.

CHAPTER TWO

THE GRANDPARENTS' GENERATION

The farms of my two grandfathers were in *la cañada de los Duranes*, east of Terromote and about seven miles from Sapello. Terromote occupied only the valley alongside Highway 94. But most people called the whole area Terromote. Grandfather Sandoval had about 1,000 acres, Grandfather Perea a little over 200. Every neighbor was related in some way, and there were no Anglos. Integration has its advantages, but for us the isolation was a blessing. We had a time to develop a deep sense of who we were before we ventured out to a more conflictive world.

Enrique Perea

(Born 1866, died 1962)

Grandfather Enrique was blue-eyed, tall and heavy-set. I remember he was always working. He would be up at dawn daily and out tilling the fields by sunrise, easily the best tended and productive in the area. Although his farm was only one-fifth as large as that of his neighbor Octaviano Sandoval, he had the best harvests. He had the best horses, the best wagon and the best buggy, which he used to take his family to Mass in Sapello, the women wearing big hats. He was a talented blacksmith with his own shop, built out of logs and still standing. When the road was too muddy after a rain or the snow too deep in winter, he went on horseback. He was very religious.

Enrique and Josefita Perea.

After the noon meal, the main one of the day, he prayed the rosary while sitting in a rocking chair. After supper, he read one of several periodicals to which he subscribed, but his favorite was *La Revista Catolica*, a Jesuit newspaper published in New Mexico.

His life was well ordered, respectful and predictable. Sometimes he had a drink but always at home. During Prohibition, he made his own moonshine whiskey, according to grandson José Perea, but if he sold it he was never caught.

I do not know much about his early life, though his family lived in Manuelitas. As a youth, he accompanied his father, a blacksmith who repaired wagons, on expeditions to hunt buffalo on the plains.[1]

When Enrique was 21 years old, as he told grandson José, an orphan who lived with him at various times, his parents sat with him one day and told him, "We think you should marry. We like Josefita Vigil. Do you know her?" He replied that he had seen her in church. With his approval they approached her parents, who agreed to the marriage. Grandfather Enrique and Grandmother Josefita had four sons and two daughters: Juan, Pedro José Dolores (Lolo), Melecio, Quirina and Amada, my mother.

Grandmother Josefita.

Enrique and Josefita settled in San Ignacio, where at the beginning of the 20th century he was the manager of a large ranch. During their sojourn there, he taught in a one-room school in the nearby community Los Aguajes. I do not know whether he ever went to school, but he could read and write well enough to teach.

Josefita was from Terromote and that led Enrique to move to the area in 1917 when the ranch he managed was sold. There he built a school on his own farm to serve his family and his neighbors, including the Sandovals. The teacher usually lived in his household.

"He is the greatest man I have ever known," said grandson José Perea.[2] "He was so kind to children, teaching us all the time. He taught me how to read and write Spanish before I started school." He was a good family man, gentle and helpful. He helped my father build our home alongside Highway 94. Whenever my brothers and I went to his house, we went up to the attic. He had books there that we paged through, including one with many pictures of the skyscrapers on New York's Manhattan Island. I went through that book every time we went to the attic, wondering whether I would one day be able to visit New York, never dreaming that I would go to graduate school at Columbia University on that famous island.

In 1942 he sold his farm and moved to Las Vegas because Grandmother Josefita was sick and he wanted to be close to a hospital. After she died, several years later, he eventually married again, to a woman named Francisca, but she, too, died before him. When he was too old to live independently, my mother brought him to Brighton and he died there in the summer of 1962 at he age of 96.

Octaviano Sandoval
(Born 1871 or 1874, died 1947)

Although he was presumably born in Manuelitas, a community in the parish of Our Lady of Guadalupe in Sapello, the archdiocesan archives have no entry on the birth of Octaviano Sandoval. The 1880 census's section on Manuelitas, found at the New Mexico State Records Center in Santa Fe, shows that his father, Estanislado Sandoval, was then a 58-year-old widower. Next to his name is that of Ricarda Jimenez, described as a single woman. Below her name are the names of her two children, six-year-old Octaviano Jimenez and five-year-old Luisa Jimenez. My grandfather was therefore the illegitimate son of great grandfather Estanislado and Ricarda Jimenez. But the archdiocesan archives have no baptismal entry for Octaviano Jimenez. The 1930 census shows that Octaviano Sandoval was then 59 years old, which if correct would make 1871 his birth year. But on his tombstone, in the cemetery by the chapel of San Ysidro, his birth year is inscribed as 1877. There is much about Grandfather Octaviano that is simply unknown.

No one in the family ever referred to Ricarda Jimenez as the mother of Octaviano and therefore my great grandmother; she was simply called *la india Ricarda*. Interviewed in 2004 at the age of 92, Uncle Herman said Ricarda was his father's sister. But the sister was Luisa and there is no record of what happened to her. I do not remember my father ever referring to Ricarda Jimenez as his grandmother. The reason may be that she was an Indian or that she was not married to our great grandfather Estanislado.

Octaviano, a short, energetic green-eyed man, once had as many as 500 sheep, a few cows, goats, hogs, rabbits and chickens. He cultivated beans, corn and other dry-land crops. But he was also a contractor for mine props and railroad ties, traveling widely, which forced him to reduce his herd of sheep. At one time he also had a tract of land alongside the Cañoncito River near Manuelitas and a house in Las Vegas, where the family lived part of the winter.

Octaviano married Teodorita Cordoba, born on April 1, 1883, in Rainsville, NM. While Grandfather was ebullient and outgoing,

Grandmother Teodorita was a woman of few words. "She worked very hard milking the cows, canning corn, vegetables and fruit," remembered granddaughter Josephine. "She put the milk in big pans to make butter and cheese."[3] She smoked hand-rolled cigarettes, a practice uncommon among the women of Terromote at the time. Several of us grandchildren remember seeing her cigarette glowing in the dark while she lay in bed.

Grandparents Octaviano and Teodorita Sandoval, son Eusebio, and daughter Pablita in 1924.

Octaviano and Teodorita had 14 children, of whom 11 survived beyond childhood. They also adopted two orphans, the first being Isabel Sandoval, who fought in France during World War I and died in 1930 from the damage caused to his lungs by poison gas. "His tongue fell out before he died," Dulcinea, the youngest daughter, said. The other one was Conrado Aragon, from San Ignacio, who married Juanita, the fourth daughter. Isabel was said to be the illegitimate son of Grandpa's sister, Luisa. But Rita Vega-Acevedo, a great granddaughter who put together the family tree, speculated that Isabel may well have been my grandfather's own illegitimate son. His lifestyle gave rise to such suspicion.

Grandfather Octaviano would go to Las Vegas for a week or two of drinking and gambling. He always returned with a new dress for grandmother. "My father loved to gamble and have fun," Dulcinea said. "He was muy gustoso (very self-indulgent). He often sang Cuatro Milpas and Cielito Lindo. He loved horses. Sometimes he came home with a horse he had won in a card game."

When I was a boy, Grandfather Octaviano often hitched a ride to Las Vegas with a passing trucker. Returning tipsy, he would spend the night at our house, alongside Highway 94, rather than walk a mile and a half northeast and face the wrath of Grandmother Teodorita. One of those times, when my brother Antonio and I were perhaps seven and eight years old, he brought a bottle of whisky and, when my mother and dad were not looking, passed the bottle to us and said: "Have a drink." The next day we could not go to school because we had a blinding headache. Mother was furious, and never quite forgave him.

"I loved my father even though he was quite strict," Dulcinea, his youngest daughter, said.[4] "I remember combing his hair while begging that he let me go to a dance. When I received letters from boys, he had me read them to him. Then he asked my older sister Elis to make sure I had not left out something important. I did not like that but later appreciated his concern and interest in my life. There was no doubt in anyone's mind that he was the head of the family."

When his sons and daughters went to a dance, they would kneel before Octaviano and ask for his blessing, a common practice at the time. "For the first six years of our marriage, we lived in the house of my father-in-law," Dora Lucero Sandoval said. "He was always scolding us. He would act very angry but then he would wink his eye at you. He scolded his daughters-in-law the same as his sons and daughters."[5] Family members had derogatory names for one another and for their neighbors, a practice my father applied to us. Grandfather Octaviano's was a chaotic household, in contrast to the serenity of the Perea home. My mother said she was miserable when, in the early years of her marriage, she lived in Grandpa Octaviano's household.

At the same time, Grandpa Octaviano was a devout Catholic, belonging to the Penitentes, a penitential society of uncertain origin always strong in rural communities in New Mexico. "He taught me how to pray," Dulcinea said. "He knew many prayers, some of which I still recite today. He and my mother had a little altar in the house. Every night the whole family knelt down and prayed the rosary. Sometimes when I was a child I hid under the bed to avoid kneeling. My father was especially devout during Holy Week, when the Penitentes have special penitential services. I loved to pray the Stations of the Cross with him. He taught me how to read Spanish; my parents knew little English.

"My father was resourceful and enterprising; he loved to sell things," Dulcinea continued. "At local religious fiestas–Santiago, Santa Ana and Our Lady of Mt. Carmel–he had a little stand where he sold refreshments. In the 1920s, he also had a little store in Las Vegas where he sold wood, kerosene for lamps and food staples. My sisters Carolina and Ignacita helped at the store. At the ranch he planted wheat, beans, corn and oats and had a big garden. I still marvel at how good he was in growing things. In the front of the ranch house, he planted fruit trees that are still standing–apple trees, pears and plums."

When two sons, Octaviano Jr. and Benjamin, expressed an interest in music, he hired a man in Manuelitas to teach them how to play the guitar. They in turn taught the youngest son, Alfonso, and perhaps even their brother-in-law Geraldo Martinez (Elis's husband), for he was also a musician. They used to play at local dances. The musical tradition passed to the next generation. Celestino Aragon, Conrado's oldest son, had a band in Los Angeles. Arsenio Sandoval, son of Eusebio, learned how to play the guitar and the mandolin with tutoring from Uncle Geraldo, and, after his retirement as a teacher, wrote his own songs, which he sometimes sang on one of the radio stations in Las Vegas.

Octaviano never had a car or truck or learned to drive. In the 1940s when son Octaviano Jr. bought a Model-A pickup, Grandpa started it up and ran it into a fence, breaking several posts.[6] He died on May 3, 1947, at the age of 76, in a truck accident while returning from one of his trips to Las Vegas. Inexplicably, along a straight stretch of Highway 518, the truck, loaded with sacks of oats, turned over. Grandpa Sandoval was riding on top of the oats and some of the sacks fell on top of him. With help from sons Alfonso and Herman, grandmother Teodorita remained at the ranch until the early 1950s, when she went to live with Ignacita, then working at a restaurant in Brighton and later as a housekeeper for the parish priest in Greeley, CO. Grandma Teodorita died there in 1956 at the age of 73 and was buried there.

Casimira Aragon

(1903-1991)
An oral history: 1977
(She was a sister of Grandmother Josefita)

I was born in Terromote and grew up there but also lived two years in San Ignacio with my oldest sister, Josefita. I knew only one of my grandparents. His name was José Dolores Abeyta, who lived in the *Cañada del Rocio*. He was a musician and when I got married he and his son played. He was very tall, fair skinned, with freckles. He was a Spaniard. He liked to tell us scary stories about ghosts and witches. I re-member one night when I was 13 years old he scared us so badly that the next day he had a stomach ache from laughing so hard. He must have been about 70 years old then. He died in Las Vegas in 1922 from a fall that broke his hip.

My father was José Dolores Vigil. At first he lived in Cañoncito, but he moved to Terromote when he found he could homestead part of a land grant. He put up a few buildings and fenced the land and the land became his. That is where I was born.

We never suffered poverty. My father planted wheat, barley, oats and corn. He made and sold railroad ties and mine props. He took them to a place they called *el Azul* (near Las Vegas). We always had meat. We had pigs, cows, goats, chickens and even a few sheep. We took the livestock to graze in the sierra in the summer.

I am the youngest of 13 children, but only six lived, five girls and

Great grandparents Nieves and José D. Vigil, Seferino, Lola and Casimira, on her father's lap.

one boy: Josefita, Rosenda, Manuelita, Seferino, Lola and me. The others died of diphtheria and smallpox. There were no vaccinations then. I am the only one still alive, 74 years old. Seferino moved to Las Vegas, then to Brighton, CO, where he died in an auto accident at 42 years of age. He left 12 children, the oldest only 16. The lights went out on his car and it was hit by a truck. Josefita, the oldest, lived in San Ignacio and Terromote. Rosenda lived in Rociada, Manuelita in Trinidad (CO), and Lola lived all her life in Terromote, right there where Eusebio´s family had their farm.

My father used to take me with him to cut pine trees for mine props. He pulled one side of the saw and I pulled the other. I must have been about 15 years old then. We worked until I was ready to throw up from fatigue. So I used to escape to stay with my sister in San Ignacio.

Our parents took us to Mass every Sunday in Sapello. We went by wagon or buggy. Every night after supper, we got together and prayed the rosary. My father led us in singing hymns and for Lent he read the Passion. We had to give the responses. For Christmas we lit luminarias and prayed together.

I used to walk more than a mile to a one-room school in Peñasco. I also went to a school in San Ignacio during the two years I lived with my sister and to one in Terromote. I remember the teacher was named Rafael. I learned to read and write there, both in Spanish and English, and to do arithmetic.

Dario and Casimira days before wedding in 1919.

I hardly knew my husband, Dario Aragon, before I was married, but he was a very good man, good to me and to everyone else. He was not too tall, about five feet six inches. He made mine props and farmed. I met him at a dance. I had gone with Juan Perea (her nephew) and Juanita (his wife). Afterwards, Dario started writing letters to me, saying that he liked me and wanted to get married. But when World War I started he was drafted into the Army. He did not get to Europe because on the way over everyone got the measles and the ship turned around and came back. Shortly after that, the armistice was signed. But my Compadre Filadelfio (Aragon) did go overseas. We continued writing letters and when Dario was discharged he wrote asking if I would marry him and I wrote saying yes.

Soon afterward we were startled by a long line of wagons and buggies coming up the road to our house. We thought maybe they were coming to go to confession because the parish priest was there. He used to come on horseback to say Mass at the local chapel and stayed overnight at our house. But a nephew named Milnor, Rosenda's son, about 10 years old, guessed why they were coming and teased me by singing a wedding song.

My father banished me to the kitchen and welcomed the visitors, who had come from Las Dispensas (about 15 miles away). They talked for a while about different things and then two of them stood up and said: "Our purpose in coming is to ask for the hand of your daughter Casimira to marry Dario." My parents gave no response and the visitors finally left. Then my father summoned me and asked: "Do you want to get married?" I said I did. So about 15 days later he and Enrique Perea (his son-in-law) went to Las Dispensas and said the answer was yes. I did not know they were doing this and, after they came back I said to my father: You should at least have told me.

Sometime after that the family of the groom came for the prendorio (engagement) and to get the dowry. We had a dinner with a lot of wine and everything was beautiful. That was on a Saturday and the following day we just sat under the pines and talked. The following day we were married in San Ysidro. We came back to our house for the fiesta with a wedding march, music, lots of food and dancing. For our wedding night we went to a house owned by Enrique. We stayed there for two days and then Dario and I went to Las Dispensas by wagon. It was covered but a fierce rain made us sopping wet. They were waiting for us with music and a big fiesta. That was in 1919; I was 16 years old.

We moved into a one room cabin Dario had built. It needed only plaster. We lived there until he could build a kitchen, which he made from railroad ties. After two years we returned to Terromote. My father needed someone to help on the farm. We lived there very comfortably until we acquired a big debt and had no money with which to pay it.

During Prohibition (1919 to 1933), Dario made moonshine whiskey to supplement our income from the farm. We were able to buy a new car and had just paid it off. One day he took five gallons of whiskey to Terrero (in the mountains upstream from Pecos). He had telephoned the buyers (probably copper miners) to let them know he was coming. A policeman was waiting and arrested him. It was politics; everyone made moonshine. He was fined $250 and had to go to court in Las Conchas, where his car was confiscated. We had no money to pay the fine and had to borrow from a neighbor.

That is why Dario went to work as a miner in Terrero while I stayed behind, living in a little room Carolina Padilla offered me in her house. They had moonshine whiskey in her house too. One night an old car drove up and some men got out. They yelled: "Open the door. We want to buy some whiskey." Behind the locked door I shouted that we did not have any. They replied that if I did not open they would break down the door and blow up the house. So I took a rifle and fired two shots through a crack in the window. You should have seen them run (laughter). I fired over their heads to frighten them. After that I was able to join Dario in Terrero. He worked there for about a year. We lived in cabins the mining company had for the workers.

At that time, I was not afraid to fire the rifle or the pistol we had, something I could not do now. Later when we lived in Manuelitas we had several apple trees, but the boys in the neighborhood liked to climb the trees to steal the apples. One evening I heard them and told them to stop, but they ignored me. So I fired two shots and they fell out of the trees, terribly frightened.

When we returned from Terrero we planted all the land and harvested much barley, wheat and oats. But early one afternoon a fire started in a haystack and burned everything. We had just threshed the grain and brought in the hay. Dario and I had to run through the flames to push the wagon out of the barn. We had to buy hay by the bale.

After that we lived two years on a rented farm in Manuelitas. That is when Dario decided to come to Colorado. We could not live in Terromote because we had had trouble with the neighbors and the farm in Manuelitas was not ours. *(Continued in Chapter Six)*

———

[1] Amada Sandoval interview with author.
[2] Author's interview of Jose Perea, 2004.
[3] Author's interview of Josephine Jacquez, 2003.
[4] Lucy Branch's interview of Dulcinea Olivas, 2005.
[5] Author's interview of Dora Lucero Sandoval, 2004
[6] Author's interview of Josephine Jacquez, 2003.

CHAPTER THREE

THE SONS AND DAUGHTERS

O f Grandfather Enrique's sons, Pedro worked as a shepherd and track laborer most of his life, in Utah, Colorado and Arizona. Juan worked in the copper mines in Terrero, near Pecos, while his wife, Aunt Juanita, and her five children remained on grandfather's farm. A foreman, he was once trapped for three days when a mine shaft caved in. But rescuers drilled a hole to provide air and food. During the time that he worked in Terrero, which is only about 50 miles from Terromote, he fathered three children with the nurse of the mining camp physician. Few people knew about his second family until 30 years after his death; a son, then living in California, visited José Perea in Sapello and told him about it.[1] Uncle Juan contracted tuberculosis and died in 1939.

Juan Perea, a miner, oldest son of Enrique Perea.

José Dolores (Lolo) also worked as a miner in Terrero, as a cook at the state mental hospital in Las Vegas, and as a deputy sheriff in San Miguel County. Like his older brother, he too contracted tuberculosis in the mines but survived. Melecio was a policeman who rose to the rank of chief of the West Las Vegas Police Department and then was elected sheriff of San Miguel County in 1970 and died while in office (see below). Quirina married Filadelfio Aragon and he had a farm alongside Grandfather Perea's. They moved to Colorado in 1942 and settled in Brighton. Like her husband, she died in an accident, an auto collision. Amada (see below), the younger daughter, married Eusebio from the adjoining Sandoval ranch and they gradually acquired more than 200 acres of land alongside Highway 94. They moved to Brighton in 1944.

Of the six Sandoval daughters, Pablita, born in 1902, played a pivotal role in the destiny of the family. She married a Lebanese man named Sam Alle, born in 1895, who came to the United States from Beirut, Lebanon, when he was 15. He came alone as a stowaway on a ship, according to brother-in-law Herman Sandoval. He had a cousin in Uniontown, PA, but ended up in Wyoming, where he went to work as a section hand for the Union Pacific Railroad. When he expressed the desire to marry, a fellow worker told him, "I know a man in New Mexico who has many daughters. Would you like to meet one?" Alle went to Terromote, met Pablita, returned to Wyoming, courted her by letter and later came to marry her in the parish church in Sapello. They moved to Wamsutter, WY, a village of about 100 people, the crews for two sections of railroad and their families, living in crude houses provided by the railroad: no running water, inside plumbing, just "two holer" pit privies in the back.

In the cultural tradition of Arabic people, Alle was an entrepreneur, equipping shepherds, cowhands and railroad workers. Eventually he even built small houses in Rawlins for railroad laborers. Whenever there were work opportunities, as shepherds, cowhands or railroad workers, he notified his brothers-in-law in Terromote.

Uncle Conrado and my father, born in 1904, were the first to go there to work as section hands on the Union Pacific Railroad. My father went up at least one more time during the Great Depression but was unable to find work on the railroad and had to work as a shepherd, living in a covered wagon he drove from place to place following the herd. He was there for almost a year. I remember the day he came home sick with some kind of fever, determined not to do that kind of work again.

On one of those trips to Wyoming, Herman, then only 17, went along with Conrado and Eusebio. Uncle Sam Alle sized them up and decided my father and Uncle Conrado were strong enough to work on the railroad. He found Herman a job herding sheep, familiar work because Grandfather Octaviano had many sheep. Unlike my father, Herman loved working with sheep and never worked on the railroad. He worked in Wyoming several times, but always returned to Terromote, where he eventually bought or inherited most of the land owned by his siblings and parents.

My father, Eusebio, attended school only sporadically, always having to drop out to help on the farm, and never got beyond the fifth grade. But he had a deep desire to learn and, as a farmer, regularly stopped at the county Extension Office to pick up booklets on soil conservation, on raising livestock and on food preservation. Moreover, he was very confident of his ability. One bitter winter during the Great Depression when we ran out of meat, he borrowed a gun from Aunt Juanita Perea to hunt deer. Having little faith that he would be successful, she gave him only three shells. But he killed a large buck with one shot and returned the other two shells. When he left the ranch, he worked mainly as a laborer but eventually founded a successful landscaping business in Denver. He died in 1981 shortly before his 77th birthday.

Uncles Benjamin and Octaviano Jr. settled in Kansas City after serving in the Army during World War II. Benjamin, a former military policeman, worked for Columbia Steel Tank Manufacturing Co. as the owner's driver and bodyguard as well as caretaker for his estate. Octaviano Jr. worked for the Santa Fe Railroad. They had their own band, which played at dance halls in Kansas City and had a loyal following. Alfonso worked as a track laborer in Colorado and Wyoming after he left the farm.

Of the daughters, Ignacita never married, working most of the time as housekeeper in a parish, the last one in Greeley, CO., where she died. Carolina married Apolinario Padilla and except for a sojourn in Oakland, CA, during World War II, lived out her life in New Mexico, as did her sister Elis, wife of Geraldo Martinez. Dulcinea, the youngest, moved to Colorado with her husband, George Olivas, where he worked at Rocky Mountain Arsenal destroying old chemical weapons.

Amada Perea Sandoval

(1911-1997)

[Amada, my mother, wrote this memoir for me in the late 1970s, in longhand.]

I was born in New Mexico in 1911 in San Ignacio, a beautiful place at the foot of Hermit's Peak, about 20 miles northwest of Las Vegas. There the sun hides behind the peak early in the afternoon and you can't see the sunset. But you can see the beautiful colors in the sky in the evening.

My father worked for a very kind rich man with a big farm named José Lujan. He was in charge of everything, cattle and the men who worked there. We had a big house with three bedrooms, a kitchen, dining room, a long hall and a big family room my mother used for guests. Two orchards provided us with lots of fruit. But at the end of nine years, Mr. Lujan died and the

Amada and Quirina.

farm was sold. So daddy bought land, close to grandpa and grandma Vigil 15 miles northeast of San Ignacio in a place called Terromote.

We bought 200 acres for $2 an acre. Since there was no house on the land, my father built two cabins 12 feet apart. In between he built two walls and made another room we called *el zaguán* (entrance hall) and used as a bedroom. One cabin was 20 x 20 feet divided into a kitchen and dining room, the other 18 x 18 feet where my mother had two beds and a little one for my brother Melecio. In one corner we had a wood stove. We called this the big room.

We moved to Terromote early in the spring of 1917. Melecio was born on June 17 of that year. I was then six years old. My father had to break the ground to plant seeds for 10 acres of wheat, eight acres of oats and about 15 acres of corn. The soil was good, producing good crops. On a level patch by the arroyo my mother planted carrots, lettuce and radish. In front of the cabins, she planted two cherry trees and gooseberry bushes.

At first, prairie dogs ate the wheat as it was coming up. We did not know what to do. But one day my father went to town and met a friend who promised to help him. In a week or so, he came with a sack of poison oats and in two days the prairie dogs were gone forever.

The land my father bought was dry. He and my brothers had to dig two wells, very hard work because the water table was too deep. But they found water for the animals and for our use. In spite of all the hard work, we were very happy in our own place. Sometimes my father took a wagonload of wheat to town and got enough flour to last the winter. Sometimes he and Mama took a load of corn and she bought shoes for us children. It was a happy day when Mama went to town because she brought all kinds of goodies. We waited anxiously for her to come home. My older sister Quirina and my brothers Lolo and Melecio stayed home and took care of everything. We were expected to do all the work around the house while Mama and Papa were away.

I did not start school until I was eight years old because the school was two miles away. But my father and all the neighbors applied for a permit to build a schoolhouse on our farm. It had only one room, but it could hold 20 students. The state provided a teacher. During my first year, I learned to read in Spanish and in English. My father asked my teacher to teach me both at the same time.

When we had lived on our farm three years, my father built another cabin for his blacksmith shop. During the winter when the weather was fair, he worked in his shop. Sometimes he made rings for us. Another time he made a merry-go-round that was fun to ride. But when the weather was bad, he stayed inside reading and fixing shoes. In the afternoon, he chopped wood and fed the stock. When it was cold, Quirina sat by the fire and sewed clothes for my dolls.

We had no radio or television or even a telephone, but we had other things to enjoy. When I was 11, I started riding the horses. By the time I was twelve I was helping my brother round up the cattle. I could saddle the horse and put on the bridle. We had a small horse we called pony. Sometimes a family had a dance and we all danced. On Sunday the children got together and jumped rope or played baseball. My brother and a neighbor boy made guitars out of square tin cans and sat on top of a little hill playing and singing. Sometimes my father took us up to the high ridge we called *el fragoso* (the rugged land) for a picnic. One time after a winter storm, my father built a sleigh to which he hitched a team of horses and we went to my grandma and grandpa's to pick up the mail. My grandma was glad to see us and gave us a piece of pie and some biscochitos. For Christmas she visited my uncle Seferino and brought back candies, nuts and apples for us. Those were the good old days for me when we did not worry about bills.

In 1921 when Quirina got married, Mama told me I had to do all the things she did. I washed dishes morning and night and the wooden floors once a week with a brush and a piece of homemade soap. I also fed the pigs. Mama got me up early in the morning to hold the bucket for my dad as he milked the cows. I did not like that, but I had to obey.

The church was eight miles away. In the winter we went only when the weather was good. When it was bad, my father went by himself on horseback. In the springtime when it was windy and dry, the neighbors got together to pray for rain. We walked around the fields praying the rosary and then stopped in a house for coffee, cookies or pie.

Mama was always very busy. During our second year on the farm, she built an earth oven (horno). In that oven we baked bread and many other things. We used it every year to make chicos (corn roasted, then dried) when the corn was ready to eat. In those days we dried all our vegetables and never bought them in cans. My brother Lolo took care of the cows providing us with milk. The rest of the cattle were up on the ridge behind our farm.

We got most of our food from the farm, having to buy only coffee, sugar, potatoes and a few other necessities. Kerosene for the lamp cost about 60 cents a month. We visited the doctor only when seriously sick. For colds we had home remedies. I helped my mother pick herbs to save for the winter.

Springtime was the season I liked best, when everything was getting green. The month of May was the most beautiful. The family gathered in the big room to pray the rosary and sing hymns to Mary. The fall was beautiful too, when we gathered the harvest, including a pile of corn ready for husking, and the pigs were fat with our winter meat. Around November when it was cold enough to hang the meat up in the attic, we butchered a pig and, sometimes, a calf. Then people from Española came with chile and apples to trade for wheat, meat and even yellow peas. My father always traded with them. Sometimes, too, he took a load of firewood to Buena Vista, about 15 miles away, and brought back plums, carrots and some other vegetables. Some winters, men from southern New Mexico came by with piñon nuts my father bought with wheat. On winter nights we sat by the stove eating the piñon nuts and telling spooky stories about witches.

There were times in the spring when my father was so busy he could not go to town and we ran short on food. That is when Mama decided to kill some of the old hens, the ones not laying eggs. But we always had lots of eggs; so it was never too bad.

My grandma lived about two miles away. We visited her very often; she was a wonderful person. She was always happy to see us and always had something good for us. I used to stay with her for a week or two in the summer. In 1925, when I was 14, I stayed with her during the winter and went to school in Peñasco with a German teacher named Ella Klecke. She was a wonderful person and I learned a lot from her. I was in the 6th grade and she advanced me to the 7th. My brother Lolo went to school with her too. Grandma packed a lunch for me and José, a little orphan grandson in the first grade. Because he was little, I held his hand as we walked to school.

In 1926 another German teacher came to teach at the little school on our farm, paying room and board at my sister Quirina's house. Lena, only 20 years old, and I had lots of fun together. My sister and brother-in-law, Filadelfio Aragon, took us to dances. She did not date and I did not either; my parents were very strict. But they were good parents. All I know and all I have been I learned from my parents. The good example my mother gave me has helped me to be a good wife and mother. She has been gone for many years, but in my mind she still lives.

In April 1926 I got a letter from a neighbor boy working in Wyoming. He said he was interested in me and thought I was a very good girl. He hoped that one day I would be his wife. I did not know what to do. I did not want to answer, but I talked to my sister and she said there was nothing wrong in replying. In my letter I told him I was in the 7th grade. We wrote to each other for more than a year. We did not date but after he came back from Wyoming we sat together, talked and danced at family dances. We were married on June 20, 1927, when I was 15 years and nine months old.

Amada and Eusebio on their wedding day. She was 15.

From June 20 to Aug. 11 we lived with my father-in-law's family. Then we got a cook stove and they lent us the use of a room about 15 x 12 feet. There we had a bed, a table and the stove. Having no place to put my dishes, we used two orange crates. That November my husband caught a very bad cold that turned out to be rheumatic fever. At that time, my parents-in-law had a house in Las Vegas where they spent the winter. There they set up a little store. Herman, my brother-in-law, and Juanita, my sister-in-law, went with them so they could go to school in town. The rest of the family stayed at the farm. But when my husband got sick, my father-in-law took us with them so my husband could go to the doctor. We stayed four months in town and I became very homesick for my mother and family. I wanted to go back to the farm so badly that in March my father and mother went for us. We stayed two months with them, then went back to my father-in-law's farm.

My husband was getting better and I was four months pregnant with my first baby. We lived there until June 15 and then went to live with my parents again. We stayed all summer because my mother wanted me to stay with them until the baby came. Antonio was born on Aug. 8, 1928, when I was almost 17 years old. In September my father-in-law asked us to come to live with them. We had a stone house with three rooms across a little lake from theirs.

In September 1929, Antonio died and six months later Moises was born. Then 18 years and seven months old, I was very happy with him;

he was my consolation and the grief for my other baby started to fade away. I was so afraid that he too would get sick and die that I would not leave him for a minute. My husband was not there when Moises was born because he had gone to Wyoming to work on the railroad. He wanted to earn money to buy sheep. After nine months, when Moises was six months old, he came back. I had saved all the money he sent to me. From a man in Rociada, we bought 22 head of sheep and put them with my father-in-law's flock.

My father gave me 17 acres of land and we began farming. The first year we planted 3-1/2 bushels of wheat and harvested 53-1/2 bushels, enough to trade for flour for the winter. The rest we sold to buy food, shoes and clothes. On July 19, 1931, my third son, Antonio, was born. My husband was then planning to buy some more land. One day his grandpa came over. He said he was getting quite old, having difficulty taking care of his land, and offered to sell us 210 acres at $2 an acre, adding it was good farming land at a cheap price. My husband liked it and we bought it. It was by the highway. Then I traded my 17 acres for 36 acres my father-in-law had by the highway adjacent to what we had bought from grandpa. We gave my father-in-law the 17 acres and 16 sheep for the 36 acres. We then had 246 acres but no house.

In January 1933, my father and my husband started building a log cabin for us, putting the roof on by February 2 and finishing everything by May. We moved in and brought with us 20 hens and nine baby pigs and their mother. We were so happy to have our own place. The cabin was 20 x 20 feet. Arsenio, my fourth son, was born there on June 13. Since we had only one horse, we traded eight sheep for another one. We no longer had to borrow one from my father-in-law. One was Bob and the other Kido, so gentle I used to ride him around the farm.

In 1935, my sixth son, Elivinio, was born. That summer my husband bought four goats to provide badly needed milk for the children. I often made cheese. In the spring of 1936, we added another room to the cabin, this one made of stone. Again my father helped us. The family was growing and we needed another bedroom. It was about 20 x 18 feet and I could set up three full beds. By that time we were doing much better; the crops were good, we had our own meat, vegetables from the garden, eggs from our chickens and plenty of milk. We sold our remaining sheep and got cows.

In July 1937, when Carmel, my seventh son, was born, I began wondering if I would ever have a girl. In August 1939, when Raymond, my eighth son was born, my husband decided to buy a gasoline-powered washing machine. It was too hard for me to wash so many clothes by hand. He went to town with only $25, put it down on a new washer he bought for $86 at Montgomery Ward, a lot of money in those days. We paid the rest in monthly payments. I was so happy I could wash lots of clothes in a short time.

In 1942, my ninth son was born and we named him Eusebio after my husband. With the Second World War going on, people were moving to California to get good jobs. But we stayed until 1944, when we moved to Colorado. Moises, our oldest son, was ready for high school. The closest one was 20 miles away and there was no bus to get there. So that winter my husband went to Colorado and got a job at a packinghouse. We stayed until May, when we rented our farm to Herman, our brother-in-law. At midnight on Memorial Day, we boarded a train crowded with soldiers. There was no place to sit and I was pregnant again and carrying two-year-old Eusebio Jr. But the soldiers made room for us. A soldier held four-year-old Raymond; the rest stood.

We arrived in La Junta at 7 a. m., taking another train to Denver at 9 a. m. and finally arriving in Brighton at 6 p. m., where my husband was waiting for us. We stayed with my sister Quirina for two days while we looked for a place to live. We had trouble; people were afraid of us because we had so many children, but we found a very small place (two rooms) on Ninth Avenue where we lived for 10 months. The children worked all summer on the farms picking peas and beans and we saved all their earnings. In September they started school right away. Lucy, my first girl, was born on Sept. 2.

[Our first home in Brighton was a faded yellow shack. The kitchen was tiny, about seven feet square, and the sleeping room was hardly larger than the master bedroom of a low-priced suburban home. We slept wall-to-wall, so to speak, some of us on the floor on thin, lumpy mattresses we brought from New Mexico and the others on the three beds crammed into the room. A kerosene lamp provided flickering light. We shared a smelly, fly-infested pit privy with three other families. The coal stove was so corroded the ashes kept falling to the floor through holes and cracks. We drew water from a well with a hand pump. It may or may not have been potable.]

In March 1945, we bought a house on Eighth Avenue for $1,500 with a down payment of the $500 I had saved by then. It had two bedrooms upstairs and one in the basement. It was dirty and needed paint-

Eusebio and Amada at daughter Cathy's high school graduation.

ing, but we made it comfortable with a good cleaning and a new paint job. It had a big yard and we planted a good garden. My husband then quit his job on the railroad and went to work on the farm where the children worked in the summer.

In 1947 we sold our farm in New Mexico and bought a big 1-1/2 ton Studebaker truck. Because no one could drive it, we had to have a relative drive it home from the dealer. But, little by little, our son Moises learned, got his license and then taught my husband and his brothers. We used it to get to the farms to work and to haul beets to the sugar factory at harvest time.

In 1948, our oldest son Moises finished high school and went to business school for one year, then got a job in the mountains. It was a hard time for us, but he helped us until he was 21 years old. Then my husband said, "You have helped us enough. If you want to go to college go ahead." Moises then went to Colorado State University in Fort Collins for one year and then moved to Marquette University in Milwaukee, WI., where he finished. All the children finished high school and one after another went away to college and one after another got married.

Amada and Eusebio in the 1970s.

In 1950 we sold our house on Eighth Avenue and bought another one with five acres south of Brighton, right at the edge of town. We farmed the land for six years. Then we sold the land because the city grew over our land and the taxes went up. We kept our house and one-third of an acre.

In 1951 when my son Frank was born I was 40 years old. In 1955, Cathy, my last child was born; I was then 44 years old. My husband was then working for a company making fences, but in 1959 he decided to start his own business cleaning yards and mowing lawns. We made enough money to live very comfortably. By then only two children remained at home, Cathy and Frank, and both later married. In 1980, Cathy graduated from the University of Northern Colorado and that was the last graduation we had in the family.

At this time, I have 29 grandchildren and two great grandchildren.

Melecio Perea

(1917-1972)

A profile

In the humble house built in Manuelitas by Encarnacion Perea, brother of my grandfather Enrique Perea, sits an old phonograph, the proud possession of Encarnacion's daughter Agustina and her niece Mary Ann Perea. Agustina is 88, and Mary Ann is in her 60s. If you ask them, they will play the record of a *corrido* written about Melecio Perea after he died on January 17, 1972, while serving as sheriff of San Miguel County. They are the keepers of the memories of the Pereas, including a formal portrait of our great grandfather Juan Perea and our great grandmother Quirina Romero. Without doubt their proudest memory is that of Melecio Perea. The song, in Spanish, is about the community's loss of a good friend.

Sheriff Perea.

The sentiments expressed in the corrido were those of the populace of Las Vegas and of San Miguel County, where Perea had been sheriff since 1970. In a 2002 article in *La Herencia* magazine, Maurilio E. Vigil wrote that Perea was no ordinary man and no ordinary lawman. I knew him, of course, as my Uncle Melecio, who at every family wake kept us laughing deep into the night with an endless string of funny stories. As he told each one his dark brown eyes shone with glee. He was an irrepressibly cheerful man.

As a lawman, he never carried a gun on his person, only in the glove compartment of his cruiser. When he approached a house harboring someone who had to be arrested and brought to jail, he would call him out by name, tell him he had to take him in and ask him to come out.

And when the suspect came out, he usually put him in the backseat of the police car without handcuffing him. A lawman with great pride in his job, Perea could not hide his compassion and humanity. There was a veneer of humor and good cheer in everything he did.

When Perea died suddenly of a heart attack at the age of 54, he received one of the most historic funerals in northern New Mexico. Vigil quoted the Jan. 21, 1972, article in the Santa Fe New Mexican, as follows:

"With pomp befitting the highest ranking lawman of San Miguel County, Sheriff Melecio Perea was buried yesterday after a funeral Mass at historic Our Lady of Sorrows Church. The sheriff's body was carried from the church to the cemetery in a horse-drawn wagon, with members of the Junior Sheriff's Posse riding at each corner of the caisson carrying the New Mexico and U.S. flags. State, county and city police officers from all parts of the state made up the honor guard, standing at salute as the body was transferred from the church to the caisson to the grave. Twenty law enforcement vehicles, two abreast, with their red lights flashing, led the funeral procession. Members of the San Miguel Sheriff's Posse, mounted on horseback, escorted the casket. At the graveside stood the dead sheriff's black horse, saddled, but with a black boot reversed in the right stirrup, symbolizing the fallen rider. A seven-man squad of officers fired three shots each, over the grave, as more than 500 persons paid their last respects to their beloved sheriff."

Like many of the Pereas and Sandovals, Melecio worked in Colorado for a time. One day, in Brighton when I was about 15 or 16, he took me on one of the back streets and let me take the wheel of his car for a while. But he returned to New Mexico and joined the West Las Vegas police force as a patrolman in 1949. He rose through the ranks to become chief and for the next 20 years worked for the West Las Vegas or East Las Vegas police departments.

The last time I saw him during a brief visit to Las Vegas about 1970 he invited me to stay with him. He and my Aunt Tillie were not getting along well and he had moved to an apartment. The next morning before we went out to breakfast, he took out a bottle of whiskey and said: *"Tenemos que hacer la mañanita"* (We have to make the morning) and offered me a shot. He was not a heavy drinker, but he had his rituals with liquor and that tendency may ultimately have taken his life at an early age.

John Perea, a son of Uncle Melecio, became a policeman and, like his father, never carried a gun strapped to his body. He later served as a magistrate judge, moving to Albuquerque after his retirement.

Eusebio Sandoval

(1904-1981)
An oral history, 1977

I was born in Terromote (alongside Highway 94), not where my father's land was. That was in *la cañada*. That is what we called it. I was born in my grandmother's house, just behind where Cousin Ricardo's house is now. Today there is only a pile of dirt.

My father got his land by going away to work as a shepherd for about a year. He saved his money and brought it home. Some people had acreage in the Valle and he bought it for $50. Then with the rest of his savings he bought a horse and a new saddle. Then a neighbor became enamored of the horse and saddle and traded another piece of land for them. That is how he got the first 1,000 acres. Later, he bought another 1,000 acres.

Eusebio Sandoval at work in 1970s.

We made our livelihood there. At first my father bought cows. Then when I was 10 years old he traded the cows for goats. I herded them. After that we started to raise a few sheep and when I got married he had 500 of them. But then he became a contractor for mine props and railroad ties and had to sell half of them. I remember when the house was built and the orchard started. My father traded rabbits for the fruit trees (apples, pears and plums). When I was young a man gave us a pair of rabbits. Once we had 500.

My uncle Leandro built the house, using stone. He also built another house of logs where we lived at first. We called it a fuerte, or fort, perhaps because the Spaniards had made log houses to protect themselves. He was the only uncle I knew; he worked with my father. There was another uncle (Agustin) who moved to Colorado and had a lot of money, but I never met him.

I am the oldest of the sons, but I had three sisters who were older: Ignacita, Carolina and Pablita.

On the ranch we planted various crops and made mine props and railroad ties. We also sold animals we raised and ate others. It was a good way of making a living; we were in our culture, our territory. Spain taught us how to irrigate with ditches. Irrigation was used in Spain, Mexico and Egypt. A priest from here (Colorado) who went to Santa Fe to give a mission brought back chile, onions, potatoes and the technology of irrigation.

I was 10 years old when I went to school for the first time. It was the school near where Nazario Quintana lived (called Terromote school). My mother had taught me to read in Spanish before I started, but I had learned to read by memorizing, not by sounding out the letters. One day my sister Carolina picked up a newspaper my father received, called *El Independiente,* and began to read. I asked her:

"How do you do it?" She then taught me how to divide the words into syllables and sound them out.

We have been in this land for centuries. I get angry when they call us Mexicans and tell us to go back where we came from. At the Alamo the Mexicans gave the gringos a good beating. That is why they have always had it in for us. But I am proud that I am in my territory, even here in Colorado. The names tell the story, Pueblo, Las Animas, Florida and many other places named by the Spaniards. And our Indian ancestors have been here for 50,000 years.

Dulcinea Sandoval Olivas

(1922-)
(An oral history: 2005)

I was born in 1922 in Terromote at my father's ranch. I am the youngest daughter of Octaviano and Teodorita Sandoval. I went to the Perea school and graduated from the eighth grade with Josie and Sara Aragon and Cleo Perea. Then I went to high school in Las Vegas, but only for a short time. I boarded with Susie Chavez, one of my teachers. After that, I returned home and lived with my father until I was married and while my husband, George Olivas, was in the Army during World War II.

My mother and father had seven sons and seven daughters, but three of them, Patrociño, Clorinda, and Eliseo, died during childhood. Of those who survived, Ignacita, born in 1898, was the oldest. Then came Carolina, born in 1900; Pablita, 1902; Eusebio, 1904; Juanita, 1908; Herman, 1913; Elis, 1915; Benjamin, 1918; Octaviano Jr. (Tavianito), 1920; me, 1922; and, finally Alfonso, 1925. I am the only one still alive.

I met George, from nearby Manuelitas at a dance hall. He walked up, gave me a huge apple

Dulcinea when young.

and asked me for a dance. After that he often came up to the ranch on horseback, wearing colorful cowboy outfits.We were married in 1943. I was 21 and he was 17. Less than a year afterward, he was drafted into the Army and went off to war in Europe. I was six months pregnant with our first child, Georgia, when he left. Fortunately, he returned home safe and sound. *(Continued in Chapter Six)*

Dora Lucero Sandoval
(1928-)
(An oral history: 2004)

My father was named Pablo Lucero and my mother was Carmelita Baca Lucero. I was born in 1928 in the house in which we lived in Terromote. It had only four rooms and was made of adobe, with wood plank floors. I lived there until I was married, in 1944. I went to Terromote School, which had only one room. Its picture came out one time in *The Optic* (newspaper in Las Vegas) and I sent it to my son Alfonso in Arizona and he made a painting that hangs in the restaurant of my son Charlie. I went to school only until I passed to the 7th grade. I did not continue because I married then. I was 16 years old and my husband, Alfonso, was 19. I had one sister and one brother. My sister was seven years older, my brother less. My sister, Guadalupe Trujillo, became a school teacher. My brother, Rafael Lucero, was in Germany during World War II.

My parents taught me how to be a Catholic. My father, Pablo Lucero, had a small ranch and sometimes went to Wyoming to herd sheep. He was a very religious man, a member of the Brotherhood of Jesús Nazareno, called the Penitentes. They went to the moradas to pray and do penance during Lent. My mother cooked for the Penitentes in one of their homes. From there they took the food to the moradas in the area. The Penitentes went from one morada to another in procession on Good Friday. Those in the canyon would come to ours. The people

Dora Lucero Sandoval in 2004.

were very family oriented and friendly. We had *Las Tinieblas* (a holy week liturgy). In the dark, I would hear chains rattling and men carrying the cross, reenacting Jesus' Crucifixion.

My father and mother helped me to grow, to have respect and to live. They taught me to have respect for old furniture, to keep the house clean. We used to wash the floors on our knees with a brush.

When they butchered a pig and rendered the fat, what was left was called "la cola." My mother put it in a bucket to make soap and we used a little to wash the floors and they looked very pretty. That helped me a lot. We knew how to make soap with lye and pig fat.

When I was little I did not like Alfonso. He played the banjo and I saw him at dances. He played with Geraldo (a brother-in-law, husband of Elis) and Tavianito (an older brother). He used to tell me, "I want you to be my girlfriend," but I would get angry. One day when I was 15, I took a walk to see a cousin. On the road Alfonso and Dulcinea (an older sister) came by on horseback. I liked horses a lot. They asked me to go fishing with them. Alfonso gave me a fishing rod and I caught a fish but could not get it off the hook. Another time Tavianito and Alfonso came by in a car and stopped. "Get on, get on," Tavianito said. We went to Matias place (a little store) in Manuelitas and Tavianito went in to be with his girlfriend and left me in the car with Alfonso. We became friends and saw each other for the next year. It was a very happy time. We went to dances in Sapello and Los Martinez (near Manuelitas). Alfonso had attended another one-room school, called the Perea School, and I think he had completed the 8th grade.

In 1950 we moved to Las Vegas where Alfonso went to work in the state mental hospital. He worked there a few years and then he found work in Wyoming. He wanted to work as a shepherd but my brother-in-law, Conrado (Aragon), was working for the railroad in the same section and helped Alfonso get on as a laborer. We stayed here at first, then went with him but returned when he was laid off, as often happened. In 1958 we moved permanently to Wyoming.

In Wyoming we lived in section housing, sometimes in Rawlins but more often in sections nearby. We had only three rooms, two bedrooms and a kitchen. Alfonso and I slept in one room and the children on bunk beds in the other one. By 1969, we had 12 children, eight boys and four girls. Paul, the youngest, was only 11 months old when Alfonso died in an accident in 1970. We had been very happy. I kept our little house spotless. I got up at 4 a. m. to get the children's school clothing ready. I would wash one day and iron the next. Alfonso would come home at 4 p. m. So I started making tortillas and cooking at 3 p. m.

It is too hard to talk about the day Alfonso died. It happened about 1:45 p. m. on a winter day in Wamsutter. Alfonso used to say that it was his turn to be a flagman, but the foreman put him to work leveling track. The machine is like a truck. Alfonso was very worried because he did not know how to do that job well. He used to ask his sons, "How can I read the level well?" There was a siding to pull the equipment off the main track when the train was coming. He was accustomed to get off the machine on the side the train was not coming. But that day the machine had been turned around and he got off on the wrong side. He started to walk, thinking he was walking on the siding. A freight train, traveling at high speed, hit him. He did not see it because the track curved at that point. He did not hear it because the wind was blowing hard and he had several caps on. Fellow workers gathered what was left of him in a bushel basket. Everywhere they found a part of his body they put a little cross.

A short time later I opened the door and the foreman and his wife were there. Her eyes were red and she kept saying, "I want to tell you something." I replied, "What do you want to tell me?" I was afraid because they used to drink. So I ran away from them. But she insisted, "Child, I have to tell you something." It was then that I finally asked: "Did something happen to Alfonso. Then the principal of the school came and gathered all the children together to tell them. My husband was buried in Rawlins.

At that time, my oldest son, Alfonso, was in Vietnam and the next one, Ernesto, was also in the Army. My oldest daughter, Irene, already married, was living in San Francisco, CA., and the next one, Katie, was working in New Mexico. I got Ernesto out of the army so that he could help me as head of the household. At the time of the accident we were living in a section house near Wamsutter. The road master said I could stay there, but I decided to return to Las Vegas, where I had my mother and father. With the $75,000 the railroad gave me, I bought a big house, eight rooms, and spent the rest of it to buy food, pay medical bills and all the other costs. I could not work outside. I stayed home. We never lacked food. I bought groceries on credit and most of my money went for groceries.

All of my 12 children turned out to be very smart; I cannot believe it. Irene and Katie are social workers with master's degrees. Alfonso is an artist, a painter, who lives in Arizona. Ernesto worked as a car salesman in Santa Fe and now lives near me. Teresa is a supervisor in a school cafeteria here in Las Vegas. Rita, an artist in Santa Fe, works with her husband in a janitorial service they own. Ramon is a carpenter and lives in Las Vegas. Charlie went to Highlands for several years and now owns the Dairy Queen and Charlie's Spic and Span, a restaurant and bakery, both in Las Vegas. Rafael went to college three years on a cross-country scholarship, worked in the restaurant business for 23 years and then came to work with Charlie. The others graduated only from the eighth grade. Paul is a UPS contract carrier. Julian restores antique cars. John runs two service stations in Albuquerque. I have 54 grandchildren and great-grandchildren and one great great grandchild.

After my children grew up, I met a man with many cows and lived with him for 17 years. But several years ago, he died of a heart attack. We had gone to a casino and he had just started to play. He was 76.

Several years ago, Charlie suggested that I sell the house; the taxes were too high. I live in a small apartment here in Las Vegas. I miss Alfonso very much. It took me five years to let him go. After that I did not feel so bad. But the truth never disappears. The sadness remains in my heart and it is very difficult. It is very hard to live without a companion. You need someone to talk to. The children do not stay long.

Josie "Fefa" Aragon Montoya
(1922-)
(An oral history: 2005)

Josie "Fefa" Aragon Montoya.

I was born in 1922 on Grandpa Perea's farm. At that time, there was a house for him, one for Tia Juanita Perea (wife of Uncle Juan) and one for my mother and father (Filadelfio and Quirina Aragon). Tia Juanita was a very nice lady with five children: Cleo, Marcella, Henry, John and Della. When I was a year and nine months old I went to live with my grandma and grandpa; I don't know why. I am the oldest daughter; the other children, Sara, Teddy and Arthur.

[Although she was a granddaughter, she was reared by Enrique and Josefita Perea as one of their own children.]

Grandpa worked very hard on the farm, growing wheat, corn, oats, habas, peas and vegetables. Once we were old enough we helped weeding the beans and vegetables and harvesting them when they were ripe. Grandpa was always working. Sometimes I went to Mass with my Mom and Dad. The priest came to San Ysidro once a month to say Mass.

We lived very well in New Mexico. We did not have money, but we had a lot of food: vegetables and a lot of meat. We were never hungry. We had a big garden we watered every evening with buckets we filled in the arroyo. Grandpa had cows, pigs, a goat, chickens, ducks, turkeys and rabbits. I was very happy.

My aunt Amada was 11 years old when I was born. She was like a sister instead of an aunt; we grew up together. She was married in 1927, when I was five years old. She and uncle Eusebio had a house at his father's farm. I went there a lot when the kids were born to help her wash clothes. I was always there with her. I liked Aunt Amada a lot and she liked me.

Grandpa's house had a kitchen, a dining room, the zaguán (which had a bed) and a large room with two beds. Grandma Josefita was a very nice, but she was always sick. She had a goiter and a ball (rupture) on her stomach. I guess the most important thing Grandma taught me was to work. Once in a while we went to Las Vegas with Grandpa on a wagon pulled by horses. We went in the morning and slept there, at Uncle Lolo's house, then returned the next day. My daddy moved to Colorado in 1942, the year that Junior (one of Amada's sons) was born. He was born in the hospital and, afterward, aunt Amada stayed for a while at Uncle Lolo's. Grandpa sold the ranch about the same time and we moved to Las Vegas. There I got a job at the De Baca grocery, where Cleo also worked. After Aunt Amada moved to Brighton, Tia Juanita moved to Las Vegas. Then in 1945, after my grandmother died, I moved to Brighton with my parents.

Before he moved to Colorado, my daddy used to take us to dances in the wagon. In one I met my future husband, Joe Montoya, from San Ignacio. I think I was then 16 years old, but we did not get married until 1947, when I was 25 years old. He spent four years in the army, serving in Burma, and did not get out until 1946. Joe was the only one of his family to move to Colorado after the war. Another brother came for a time, but he went back. Joe and I had six children: Mary Lou, Philip, Danny, Shirley, Gilbert and Gerald. Joe died in 1988.

Mary Lou worked as a hairdresser for 18 years and for most of that time had her own salon. In 1985 she sold the salon and then worked as a judicial assistant to magistrates in various divisions of the court system until retirement. Philip worked for the U. S. Postal Service until he retired. Danny worked for Coors Brewing Co. for about 13 years and then for Adams County in various capacities. Shirley was a teacher. Gilbert works in the computer industry in Texas and Gerald is a truck driver.

---

[1]Interview with Jose Perea, 2009.

CHAPTER FOUR

ENRIQUE PEREA'S GIFT

In 1919 my grandfather Enrique Perea petitioned the state for permission to build a school on his farm in Terromote. That was the process in remote communities without school districts. If approved, as it was in this case, the state provided a teacher, a man or woman who at best had a high school diploma. With help from his neighbors, Perea built a one-room log building big enough for 20 to 25 students. It was called the Perea School. Its outside walls were plastered with red clay mud and, inside, whitewashed with calcimine. It had a floor of rough-hewn pine planks, two small windows, a metal roof and a big pot-bellied wood stove in the middle of the classroom.

There were two other one-room schools alongside Highway 94 in Terromote, one about two miles over rugged country to the south and another about the same distance to the north, each with the name "Terromote School." But they were too far for Perea and his neighbors, who lived in a valley one and a half miles east of the highway. There were no buses, cars or trucks to take students to the schools. Therefore Perea had had to teach Amada, his younger daughter, at home. While he made his livelihood farming and ranching and spoke only a few words of English, he had somehow learned enough to teach at one time in a one-room school in a place called Los Aguajes. My grandmother was illiterate and he did not want his sons and two daughters to suffer the same fate. Enrique Perea could not have given a greater gift to his children and to those of Octaviano Sandoval and other neighbors.

The Perea School in 1934, the year before the author started kindergarten there.

Amada received all her formal schooling there, graduating from the eighth grade. Eusebio Sandoval, my father, attended only briefly because he was alaready 15 when the school was built, his formal education ending in the fifth grade. Mom's and Dad's brothers and sisters, many of their nephews and nieces all went to the Perea School.

"I went to the Perea school until I graduated from the 8th grade," Josie Aragon remembered. "Cleo Perea (daughter of Juan and Juanita), Dulcinea, Alfonso, Benjamin, and Elis Sandoval were among my classmates. My youngest sister, Teddy, also studied there. Rebecca Herrera taught there for a long time; she used to live with us. Another teacher lived with my Mom. Ricardo Montoya (a neighbor) was another teacher, also Adolfo Perea, Grandpa's nephew and Luis Martinez. We studied history, spelling and arithmetic; the classes were in English. There were 20 to 25 students."

Enrique Perea in Brighton in the early 1960s when he was already in his 90s.

My brothers Tony, Arsenio, Elivinio and I also attended the Perea school for several years. When I started there in 1935 at the age of five, there were two stages of kindergarten, pre-Primer and Primer, each taking a year. One teacher taught everything from kindergarten through the eighth grade. When the school was closed in 1939, a big yellow school bus took us daily to a new four-room consolidated school in Rociada. By then a gravel surface had been laid on the highway, making it passable except during heavy snows.

Grandfather Perea inspired learning in other ways. He subscribed to newspapers and magazines that came to our mailbox because our house was alongside Highway 94. My mother and father read them from cover to cover before sending one of us to deliver them, but our grandfather never complained if they were dog-eared by then. When the periodicals got there, he read them aloud to Grandmother Josefita and she related the stories to other members of the family. He was an avid reader his entire life. In his early 90s when he came to live with us in Brighton, he was always reading a newspaper or a book.

His example of subscribing to periodicals in Terromote sowed an idea in my mind. Though I do not know where I discovered it, one day I saw an ad from *Grit*, a national weekly published in Williamsport, PA, looking for paperboys to sell the paper for a commission of a nickel for each one. With no libraries in the communities or in the schools, we yearned for things to read. Since we received no allowance, this was a chance to earn a little money and read interesting stories. I wrote to *Grit* and asked them to send me a few papers every week, which I began hawking to the bus driver, the teachers at Rociada and my neighbors. I do not think I ever sold more than five or ten every week, but my brothers and I read the paper avidly. The *Grit* serialized a novel titled Tenderfoot about a young cowboy and we looked forward with much anticipation to reading each week's episode. When we moved to Colorado we took the *Grit* with us and each brother in turn became the paperboy.

Eusebio and Amada with their first six sons, the author, at left, about 1941.

The Perea School, though rudimentary, gave my parents a love of learning they relentlessly instilled in their ten children. My father was a short man, as are all his children. He always told us that we should educate ourselves so we would not have to work as hard as he did. He gathered us each night–six sons at the time–at the kitchen table around a dim kerosene lamp and we did homework whether or not it was assigned at school. At first it was just learning the ABC's in Spanish, for my mother taught us how to read and write a little Spanish before we began at the Perea School. Or it might be practicing our penmanship or working out simple problems in addition, subtraction and, later in multiplication. We were too poor to have books, but there was always a dictionary in the house.

My parents were interested in learning for themselves too. They stopped regularly at the county agricultural extension office in Las Vegas to pick up booklets on gardening, home canning, curing pork to make bacon or ham, building a root cellar to preserve carrots and other vegetables during the winter, and on drying of meat, vegetables and fruit. They put all that knowledge into practice. From one of the byproducts of rendering the fat of pigs we butchered, my mother made soap. From the Soil Conservation Service Dad learned how to make small dams to prevent erosion, a big problem because all our cultivated fields were on the slopes of hills.

Mother learned how to sew and made all our overalls on a sewing machine powered by a foot peddle. On the bib she always sewed a pocket for a pencil and she always had a wooden pencil to put in it. Though sometimes desperately poor, we always had tablets, or at least some kind of paper, to write on. Mother saved the tablets after we had filled them and often showed them to relatives. She would say: "Look how smart my sons are."

Because typewriters fascinated me, my parents, though they could hardly afford it, bought me a toy typewriter that actually worked. When I was in the fourth grade, I laboriously typed some of my homework on it. Later, we got an ancient Underwood from Grandfather Perea. In Rociada, fourth and fifth grades were in the same room. The fourth grade was so easy I started doing fifth grade work as well. My teacher told my parents I could skip the fifth grade if I attended summer school in Las Vegas for six weeks.

One day, while we were cutting Ponderosa pines for mine props with a two-man crosscut saw, Dad told me he and Mom had decided I should go. He said I would live with Aunt Elis and Uncle Geraldo Martinez while in Las Vegas. I was overjoyed. I still have a postcard I sent home on June 20, 1941, addressed on my toy typewriter to Dad: "I haven't got lost in town. It is so easy to go to school. I am doing fifth grade work. I have a very good teacher." I had no trouble passing to the sixth grade in six weeks. I also learned how to ride a bicycle. It was the only summer vacation I ever had growing up on the farm.

LAS VEGAS, N. MEX
JUN 20
8:30 AM
7941

THIS SIDE OF CARD IS FOR ADDRESS

MR. EUSEBIO SANDOVAL

ROUTE 2 BOX 2

SAPELLO,

N. MEX

CHAPTER FIVE

MEMORIES OF THE GRANDCHILDREN

As the oldest of ten children, I was trained, from the time I was four years old, to be a leader in the family, to take care of my brothers and sisters, a duty I embraced so enthusiastically, my brothers used to call me "Sarge." That set the pattern for my entire life. When my brothers and I worked in the fields, I was their supervisor. When I was a fire fighter for the National Park Service during the summers while in college, I was a fore-man or the camp boss. As a soldier, I was an offi-cer, a lieutenant in the Corps of Engineers and, while in the Army Reserve, the company com-mander of a tank unit. In every job I had as a news-

Moises at age 77.

paperman, I soon moved out of the rank of reporter to become an editor. When I moved into magazines, I was soon editor of not one but several publications. When my grandfather Sandoval's land was going to be sold, I organized five of my brothers to buy half of it to-gether and became president of the corporation that manages it. Finally, when it comes to writing the history of the people of Terromote, I felt it was my job. I know no other way to be.

The other main factor in my life is that, from my earliest memory, I had a job in the family. When I was five years old I herded the goats dur-ing the summer. I helped Dad to cut the corn stalks and to stack the sheaves on the wagon to bring them to the barn. In the winter, I helped to chuck the corn. Every day I had to chop and haul wood to the house. In the summer I milked the goats with the help of one or two younger brothers. And when Dad killed a kid goat for meat I had to hold it while he cut its throat with a sharp knife. How I hated to do that! Then when Dad went to Wyoming on several occasions to work on the railroad or as a shepherd, absences that stretched for many months, I was the man of the family.

We used to work extremely hard. One day, when I was nine years old, my father and I cut 100 pine trees in half a day with a two-man crosscut saw. I was so tired I was afraid my legs would give way as we walked home. Fear of my Dad's anger made the work much harder. Another time that we were cutting Ponderosa pines for mine props, the saw grazed my leg. I was afraid to tell him, and he didn't notice it until my shoe filled with blood. The sight frightened him and he rushed me home. During harvest, my father threw the bales of corn stalks on the wagon and I had to arrange them on a wide unsteady rack; I was always afraid the load would slide off the wagon. When we made dams, I had to drive the team of horses while Dad guided the hand-held scraper. When I did not do it well he whipped me with the reins. That is why I was always happy to see him leave when he went to work in Wyoming, even though my next brother, Antonio, and I would have to do a man's work on the farm.

[However harsh my father was, he loved me in his own way. My fondest wish at that time was to have a bicycle, and he bought a new one for me, no easy feat considering our lack of money and paperwork required by the government during World War II. I was the only boy in Terromote with a bike.]

The last time he went away to work, this time to Colorado during a very hard winter and spring, he found work in a packinghouse in Denver. Then 13 years old, I had to help Mom take care of the livestock and go to school, where I was in the eighth grade. We ran short of feed for the cows and one of them collapsed. Mom and I tried every way we knew of to get it to stand up, but try as we might, we did not succeed and the cow died. We also ran short on groceries. So Antonio and I cut enough pines with a two-man crosscut saw to make a truckload of mine props. We cut the logs to various lengths, depending on thickness, and peeled them as required by the mining company. When we were finished we flagged down a trucker and arranged to have him haul the props to Las Vegas for half the proceeds from the sale. Antonio, then 12, and I went with the trucker to Las Vegas. With our share of the proceeds we bought the groceries Mom needed and gave her what was left. I weighed only 90 pounds, but I felt manly nonetheless.

Dr. José A. Perea
(1932-)
(An oral history: 2004)

My first childhood memory is of the day my mother died of tuberculosis. That was in 1936 when I was four years old. My grandfather Juan Duran had built a one-room cabin for her alongside Highway 94 in Terromote. He apparently thought that having her there improved the chances of having a passing motorist give her a ride to Las Vegas when her condition became critical. His farmhouse was in a valley far from the road. That day my brother Jacobo (Jake), who was six, and I were at my mother's bedside when my cousins Josie (Fefa) Aragon, Cleo and Marcella Perea came to visit. My mother told them: "Get them out of here; I don't want them to see me like this." The girls, teenagers, played with us outside on some swings while the grownups tended to our dying mother. I remember Fefa said: "These two are really going to suffer." My father was working as a shepherd in Wyoming; he and my mother had separated.

My mother died there by the dirt road leading to Las Vegas, where her death might have been easier but not avoidable. Tuberculosis was a great scourge; it had taken the lives of all the women in Grandfather Juan's family, my grandmother, several aunts and several uncles. Only Grandfather Juan and Uncle Maque were spared. My father did not get word of my mother's death until a month later and he did not come back to take care of Jake and me. So Grandfather Juan got together with my other grandfather, Enrique Perea, and said: "You take Jacobo; I will take care of José."

Since there was no woman in the house to take care of me, I tagged along as Grandfather Juan and Tio Maque planted, cultivated and harvested oats, hay, corn and other crops and cared for the livestock. When winter came I had no overshoes, but Grandfather Juan wrapped burlap on my feet and I played in the snow without getting wet. But since we seldom bathed, I became very dirty, had lice in my hair and my skin was cracked.

When I was five, Grandfather Juan told me, "I am going to talk to my compadre. I have to take you where there are women. They have to clean you up. It is time that you start school." I went to live with my grandfather Perea and attended the one-room Perea School on his land. He had taught school in Spanish. He had the instruction books in the attic when I went to live with him.

One day when I came home from school a Model-A car was parked outside Grandpa's house. Martin Trujillo and his wife, "la Chonita," were visiting. She was a niece of my grandmother Josefita. When I came in, Chonita was crying. She could not have children and very much wanted a child. My grandmother pointed to me and said, "Why don't you take him. He does not have anyone." They put me in the car and, when we went by the well, we hit a bump and I flew up and hit the roof. After that they held me down. They sent me to another one room school in Terromote, alongside Highway 94 near Peñasco, across a field from the Trujillo farm.

From the very first, Martin did not like me. He beat me and cursed me, threatening to take me back to Grandpa Duran. When he sent me to get water from a well across the road, he would spit on the ground and say: "If you don't get back before the spit dries, I am going to give you a beating." And he did; he punished me by making me kneel on a piece of wood with a sharp edge. As a result, I began wetting my bed at night, which upset him to the point that one day, he said: "I swear to God I am going to kill you." After that I did not sleep at night so that I would be awake to pee in the basin. I slept during the day when he was gone, working for the Works Public Administration. Chonita, however, really loved me; she taught me the catechism. She cried when Martin beat me.

Then Martin decided to go to Colorado to look for work, but we first went to Cheyenne, WY, where Chonita had a brother. Since Martin found no work there, we came to Henderson, CO, where he got a job as a foreman at a vegetable farm. *(Continued in Chapter Six.)*

Arsenio Sandoval

(1933-)
(An Oral History: 2005)

My first memory as a child in Terromote was of being taken to Peñasco school to be vaccinated for smallpox. I do not think I was yet in school. Anyway, I remember the smell of the alcohol. The memory was not completely unpleasant, but I was a little scared. The next memory is of having a little red coat and Dad taking me with him to the woods to make mine props. He got so engrossed that when I fell asleep he forgot me. I either came home by myself or he went back for me, but I remember Mom scolding him.

One day when I was about five years old, my Dad took me hunting. For that one day I was special, just he and I. He took some burlap, wrapped my feet, and we walked all the way to the end of Grandpa Sandoval's *cañada* (valley). He saw a deer, but didn't get a chance to shoot it. I did not see it. At other times, Dad was very strict. Once when my brothers were teasing me, I told them to go to hell and Dad thought I was addressing him, as he was shaving. He slapped my face, really hurting my feelings. Another time while we were working in the barn loft, he became impatient with Tony and threw a pitchfork at him, gouging his scalp and barely missing his eye. Leby, his favorite, did not get punished the way we did. Otherwise, I remember Dad as a good person, with a sense of humor, always telling stories.

Before I started at the Perea one-room school, my mother taught me how to read and write in Spanish. I remember those sessions at the kitchen table around a kerosene lamp. Mom and Dad told stories, she about Aladdin and he about lost treasures and dead people (*difuntos*). The house had three rooms, Dad and Mom's bedroom on one side, the kitchen in the middle and a bedroom for all of us six boys. We all

Arsenio in his teens.

slept in one bed. It was very uncomfortable when you were in the middle. At the school, our teacher was a woman whose name I forgot. I remember reading with some of the cousins, they making jokes about it. For the Christmas pageant, with my parents there, I had to recite something and point toward the tree, but I was too shy and undemonstrative.

I was only ready for the first grade when the Perea School closed. The next year we went to Rociada. My father alertly promoted me one grade. He told the teacher I should be in the second grade and she said ok. What I most remember there are the fierce fights we had in the playground, the boys from Terromote against those from Upper or Lower Rociada or Cañoncito. There was a boy who had a double thumb and since everyone wanted to see it he began charging a nickel for each viewing.

In the summer, Leby and I or Tony and I took care of the goats or cows. Mother made a lunch for us, sometimes a roasted leg of *cabrito* (kid goat). We were always playing. One time we started a grass fire. To keep me from coming home early, Tony would sometimes tie me to a tree. One time, when we were coming home after dark, some older boys coming from Las Vegas scared us by making sounds like a mountain lion, and we ran home. Another time we lost a goat and Dad went to look for it at night. Later we heard a knock and when we went to the door, there was Dad with the head of the goat. I guess that is all the coyotes left. The goats and cows were always getting into the cornfields and we always had a difficult time chasing them out. We worked together milking the goats and cows and, sometimes, gathering weeds for the pigs. When my father used a homemade harrow we stood on it. One time I fell and it went over me, but the ground was soft and I did not get hurt. We had a small dam where we used to go swimming. *(Continued in Chapter Six)*

Dr. Antonio Sandoval
(1931-)
(Part autobiography, part oral history: 2006)

My first recollection of my education was learning to read Spanish at home. We had a Spanish book with the alphabet and pictures of animals and objects with their names in Spanish. Reading in Spanish wasn't very difficult because we spoke Spanish at home and Spanish is a phonetic language. A specific combination of letters had the same sound in every word. Reading was very appealing to me because Mom read stories to us and also told us stories that she had memorized as a child. One of the books from which she told us stories was "*Las Minas Del Rey Solomon*" (The Mines of King Solomon).

My next memory was having a difficult time reading in English. Dad drilled me by the light of the kerosene lamp. I can still hear him saying with a heavy Spanish accent and having me repeat, "Grandmother wrote a letter to Tom." I was in first grade at the Perea one-room school on Grandpa Enrique Perea's ranch in the fall of 1938. That year a Mr. Martinez was the teacher for all grades, first through eighth. Mr. Martinez on occasion would raise his voice and express his impatience with the students. I was a very sensitive child easily intimidated. I dreaded going to the black board. In my emotional state, my mind would just turn off to learning. I failed first grade.

We spoke Spanish outside the school and English only in the classroom. One day during the lunch hour Mr. Martinez said we would have to speak English inside and outside the school. Those who spoke Spanish outside would have to go inside to study. Soon everyone was inside the schoolroom, but two of us; and we simply sat by the door silent and sullen. When those who went home for lunch arrived they would say *"Qué Pasa?"* and Mr Martinez would say, "Inside to study."

I also remember the Christmas party at the Perea School. All the parents were there and a freshly cut Christmas tree was in the room.

Because we had no electricity the Christmas lights were little candles.

Then there was the day when the Public Health nurses came to the Perea School. We knew they were coming, but as they arrived, the Sandoval brothers said, "Let's run." We ran home, but we didn't escape the vaccinations. The nurses came to our house and Mom and Dad called us out from under the beds and had us vaccinated.

In Rociada, my teacher was a young woman named Miss Bustos. She was not intimidating like Mr. Martinez, so that year I completed first grade and second. Although Miss Bustos was very gentle with us, she could also be very stern. I remember a classmate and I crawled into the classroom through an open window during recess. Miss Bustos saw us and shut the open window behind us. We couldn't open it so we were trapped in the room because the door was locked. Miss Bustos came in the classroom, had us extend our hands, palms up and struck us hard with a ruler.

I spent five years at Rociada School. Sometimes two of us were asked to go to the river to get a pail of water for the classroom. There was an orchard by the river and one day we climbed a tree to get purple plums. While we were up in the tree the owner of the orchard came by. We froze where we were while his dogs barked below us. The owner looked up to the trees but couldn't see us. He finally left and with a sigh of relief we resolved never to steal plums again.

Occasionally we had fights at Rociada School. I hated to fight, but sometimes I had to. One time I was involved in a fight and someone from the surrounding cheering crowd tossed an open knife to my opponent. When he bent down to pick it up I kicked him in the head as hard as I could. That ended the fight. Sometimes two of the Sandoval brothers were arguing on the verge of going to blows. If any stranger dared to side against one of the Sandovals, both Sandovals would turn on the intruder and pummel him with blows from every direction. It was understood that fights between Sandovals were kept in the family.

At Rociada School I saw my first movie. Because electricity was not available to run the projectors, portable generators were brought to the school. When the projectors were turned on before the picture appeared on the screen, one of the students yelled out, "*La Luna*" (the moon). We laughed about this for days.

Dad always insisted that we do well in school. Being at the top of the class was synonymous with being a Sandoval. Sometimes when I did not like a class or a teacher my natural tendency was to not try my best, but not meeting the Sandoval standard motivated me to work hard in spite of my reluctance to please a teacher. *(Continued in Chapter Six)*

Enrique Perea's Great Granddaughters

(A few of many, among whom are medical doctors, professors, teachers, a pharmacist, a systems enginner, novelist and many others.)

Mary Sandoval, associate professor of mathematics, Trinity College, B.A. Yale cum laude, Masters and PhD from University of Michigan.

Francheska Houlden, school librarian: two master's degrees.

Elena Sandoval-Lucero, PhD, past director of admissions at Metro State College and currently assistant research professor at the University of Colorado-Denver.

Rose Sandoval, managing partner, Benefits Strategy Partners, Boston. Master's in quality systems management.

Part Two: Beyond Terromote

CHAPTER SIX

LAS VEGAS, BRIGHTON AND BEYOND

When I graduated from the eighth grade in Rociada in 1944, we moved to Brighton, CO, in part so that I could go to high school. In Terromote, all schooling ended with the eighth grade because there was no school bus to take us to high school in Las Vegas. Our parents spoke English with difficulty but gradually became more comfortable. On the flyleaf of an English dictionary, Dad wrote the meaning of unfamiliar words. Toward the end of his life, he studied the Bible avidly and gladly debated the Jehovah Witnesses who regularly came knocking on the door. He welcomed them with two bibles in hand, one in English and one in Spanish. Mother also wrote songs, poems and the memoir published in this book. When Cathy, the youngest child, started religion classes in the parish, Mom volunteered as a catechism teacher.

Nine of us earned at least one college degree, something our parents never imagined when we were growing up. Dad's dreams were much more modest. He just wanted us to gain some sort of skill. Because he found shorthand fascinating, Dad hoped that I, the oldest, would become a court reporter. So he was happy when I attended business school and, after a course in shorthand and accounting, went to work for the National Park Service to help supplement the family income during a lean time.

Antonio's love was electronics and he hoped to attend the Coyne School of Electronics in Chicago. But at that point my mother's faith changed the destiny of the family. Overcoming my father's objections, she suggested he go to Regis College, a Jesuit institution in Denver. Her hope was that Tony would become a priest. Tony had no interest in the priesthood but loved science and majored in chemistry. Since I was working, I contributed a little toward his expenses during the first year, but he paid for most of them with his summer earnings as a farm worker and wages as a night orderly at a hospital, where he worked 35 to 40 hours a week throughout his career at Regis.

After my 21st birthday, when Dad said I did not have to help the family any more, I enrolled at Colorado State University, at first thinking I would be an engineer but later switched to journalism, more in line with my talents. After that, Arsenio, the third son, remembers, it was assumed that everyone would go to college. The time came when Mom began to wish she had had that opportunity. When she was 62, she told a newspaper reporter from the Denver Post who did a feature on the family: "I wish I could have gone to college. I would have studied marriage counseling, because there are too many divorces now. I would also have studied religion, because people don't know about religion."

In the early 1970s, she enrolled in classes for her GED diploma. During the several months she attended them, she was "in ecstasy," according to daughter Lucy. When she took the tests, she passed them all except for math and that kept her from getting her high school diploma. "It was heartbreaking to see her disappointment," Lucy said.

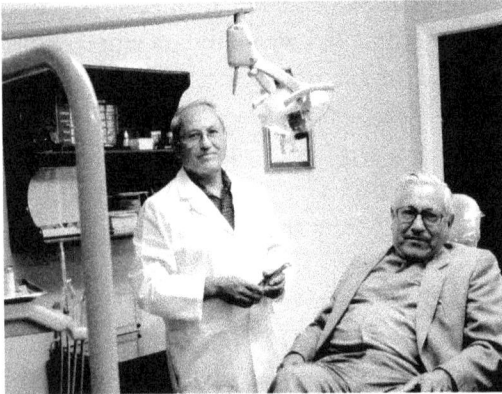

Dr. Elivinio Sandoval at his dental clinic in Aurora, CO, with his brother Antonio.

No other family from Terromote had more college graduates than Amada and Eusebio Sandoval. Antonio received a doctorate in chemistry from Kansas State University; Arsenio, a master's degree in Spanish with applied linguistics from the University of New Mexico; Elivinio a degree in dentistry from Creighton University, and, later, while in the Air Force, a specialty in periodontics; Carmel, a bachelor's degree in education from the University of Northern Colorado and graduate study toward a master's at the University of Portland; Raymond, a bachelor's degree in education from Western State College; Eusebio Jr., a master's degree in Spanish from the University of Wyoming; Lucille, a bachelor's degree in communications from Metro State College in Denver, Cathy, a bachelor's degree in business from Northern Colorado University and, later, a license as a Certified Public Accountant; and I, a bachelor of science degree in journalism from Marquette University, graduate studies in journalism at the same university, and, later, with a Ford Foundation Fellowship, a certificate in international reporting from Columbia University. Frank, the last son, had learning disabilities that doomed him to a special education curriculum, but he later became a welder, locksmith and learned a lot about computers.

Mom and Dad paid only for one college education, that of Cathy, their last child. However, they gave us something more valuable–the sense that we had good minds, the confidence that we could succeed if we worked hard, the strength to persevere. So most of us paid our own way, some with scholarships for wrestling, or for academic or professional achievement. These we supplemented with all sorts of summer and part-time jobs. In the summer, I worked for the National Park Service as a foreman on a program seeking to control white pine blister rust and as a forest fire fighter. In the winter I worked at different times as a dishwasher at a restaurant, part-time police reporter, night clerk at a freight company, part-time bookkeeper, short-order cook in the Student Union dining hall. To pay for my room, I stoked the coal furnace, mowed the lawn and shoveled snow at the home of a widow. Arsenio had a wrestling scholarship and worked on the buildings and grounds crew at Northern Colorado University. Raymond worked in construction, my Dad's landscaping business and many other jobs during the 11 years it took him to earn his degree and become a teacher, wrestling coach, and, in one school district, dean of students.

Amada and Eusebio Sandoval faced each morning with the anticipation of learning something new, acquiring a new skill, accepting a new challenge. After working most of his life as a farmer, laborer on the railroad, and even as a shepherd, he started a successful landscaping business in Denver when he was 55, communicating easily with his customers in English. He taught himself to tune up, sharpen and maintain the lawnmowers, trimmers and other machines he acquired. Mom learned how to do the billing and to keep the books for my Dad's business, using a loose-leaf notebook as a ledger.

Our parents love of learning also impressed their grandchildren. My youngest daughter, Mary, in 1994 dedicated her doctoral thesis in differential geometry, "Wave-Trace Asymptotics for Operators of Dirac Type," thus: "This work is dedicated to my grandfather Eusebio José Sandoval, to my grandmother Amada Perea Sandoval, and to my parents, Moises and Penelope Sandoval." Appropriately, she also wrote the dedication in Spanish: *"Esta obra es dedicada a mi abuelo Eusebio José Sandoval, a mi abuelita Amada Perea Sandoval, y a mis padres Moisés y Penelope Sandoval."* She received her bachelor's degree in mathematics cum laude from Yale and her master's and PhD from the University of Michigan.

My parents also inspired Anthony Raymond Alle, the son of Dad's sister Pablita and a Lebanese immigrant named Sam Alle. He used to spend months living with us in Brighton during the summer. "I remember my uncle Eusebio talking about subcontracting with the sugar beet factory to haul sugar beets," he said. "It was the first time I had heard that word."

Among Enrique Perea's great grandchildren, two have degrees from Harvard and Yale, and four are medical doctors. There is a novelist, a lawyer, an associate professor in mathematics and other college professors, a manager of corporate finance for an energy company, a pharmacist, a librarian with a master's degree, the owner of a consulting company in employee benefits, the director of the women's center at Princeton University, a pilot for an airline, a chemist, two locomotive engineers, a university director of admissions, the manager of an investment firm with extensive holdings in Latin America, many teachers and business persons, both men and women. The dividends of Enrique Perea's investment in education compound in each new generation.

Mary Perea Starz, one his granddaughters, merits special mention. She was placed in foster care along with her four siblings when Pedro Perea and his second wife, Leonor, broke up for the last time. The woman who took them in lived in Concha, AZ, where all Hispanics were placed in the vocational curriculum. Deciding they should be in the academic curriculum, she appealed to school authorities but they turned her down. Undaunted, she took the issue to the school board and won. Mary was an "A" student while her siblings were not. Eventually, with aid and encouragement from her half-brother José Perea, she earned a PhD at the University of Texas at Austin and is now a professor in the School of Education of the University of St. Thomas in Houston. Many others, as the following oral histories show, overcame daunting obstacles to educate themselves.

Casimira Aragon

An oral history: 1977
(Continued from Chapter Two)

In October of 1937 we came to Colorado to work harvesting sugar beets. Our oldest daughter Alice was then 12, George, 10, Jenny, 4, and Tony, 3. Priscilla was born here in Brighton. The first winter we lived in a rented basement that was only one room. But by the next

Casimira at age 60.

year, we were able to rent this house, which we later bought for $460. When we left New Mexico we had five cows that Dario's brother sold for $200. Then we sold our house in Las Dispensas for another $200. That is how we could buy the house.

The second summer we were in Colorado Dario got a job with the WPA (Works Public Administration) while the children and I worked on farms picking peas and beans. I continued to do this until 1946, when we worked harvesting carrots. In the meantime, Dario had worked as a janitor at Fitzsimons Army Hospital and finally at Rocky Mountain Arsenal. But one day he got a very strong pain on his right side. We went to see a Dr. Rodriguez in Denver. He said: "You need an operation, which I can do, but your insurance will not cover it."

From left, Alice, George, Casimira, Jennie, Tony and Priscilla in 1980.

On the way home, I told him: "You know (as a veteran) you could go to Fitzsimons." So we turned the car around and went to the hospital. They told him he had cancer and admitted him that very night. He came home after the operation but was never well; the cancer had spread to his liver. People told me he was *embrujado* (bewitched). I took care of him until he died in January 1945 at age 52, less than two years after the operation.

I was able to support the family with the proceeds of an insurance policy and Social Security. It was very little but Alice and George, still in their teens, were soon able to go to work. Today Alice, married and the mother of two children, works in a restaurant; George, father of three daughters, works in a meat packing house; Jennie, also mother of three daughters, lives in California, and works in Safeway; Tony, a Navy veteran and father of a boy and a girl, works in construction, and Priscilla, married and the mother of three children, works at Safeway in Brighton. I also have three great grandchildren.

There was a lot of discrimination when we first came to Brighton. There were a lot of places where we could not go. I remember one time in 1939 we went to get haircuts. They let us in but refused to cut our hair. Now it is better because young men have educated themselves and they defend us.

Arsenio Sandoval

(An oral history continued from Chapter Five)

I was 11 when we moved to Colorado. Dad was already there. We went by train, leaving Las Vegas at night. The train was crowded with soldiers. Having no place to sit, I sat on a soldier's lap. As we were coming into Denver, the city looked dirty. When we got to Brighton, 20 miles north, we went to my Tia Quirina's house on 7th Street. We started playing right away as boys do and when I had to go pee I ran into the house, but it was the wrong house and the people there threw me out.

Five of us boys started working in the fields right away, picking peas or beans for a truck farmer named (Frank) Bucci. We were fired after the first day, the farmer saying we picked everything, when we should have picked only the ripe pods. But Tia Quirina pleaded with old man Bucci to give us another chance and from then on we were more discriminating. After work we played in the neighborhood. One day I was under the city's water tank when the fire siren went off; it was like the end of the world.

We experienced discrimination for the first time. When we went to Friedman's grocery, where Mom did her shopping, one of the cashiers asked: "What can I do for you, Pancho? At the Rex Theater, we had to sit on the left side, "the Mexican section," until my brother Moises wrote a letter to the newspaper several years later and then we could sit anywhere. We had to set pins in the bowling alley because, in the winter, we could not get part-time jobs anywhere else. We also washed windows and shoveled snow. We were always going door to door looking for jobs. At St. Augustine's, the local parish, most of us became altar boys. The nuns would send us to picket the theater when it showed indecent movies, but they never went with us.

I finally got a job at Glen Taylor's grocery, where we could buy on credit. We used to run in the store, grab all kinds of candy and run out yelling, "Put it on the bill." One time he chased us around the block until he caught us. The next week, we had to work shoveling coal for the furnace at his home. One time, when he was running for mayor, he hired a guy named Arturo Naranjo and me to distribute flyers in the "Mexican part of town." We did it until we got tired and then threw the remaining flyers down a storm sewer drain.

In high school, I was very smart but very quiet, not too sociable. I took bookkeeping and shorthand. We would go to the teen canteen and wait until the end before we mustered the courage to ask a girl for a dance. The song was always, "Now is the hour when we must say good-bye." I was on the wrestling team (at 103 pounds) and got a lot out of it. I won first place in the league and went to the state tournament, the first boy from Brighton to do so. I loved it when I pinned my man and the cheerleaders would yell, "Yea Artie, Yea Sandoval, Yea Artie Sandoval."

I was inducted into the National Honor Society, the second in our family to make it, Moises being the first.

Tony, always doing science experiments in the basement, was the first one to go to college. By the time my turn came, I was expected to go. But, also, with the Korean War going on, I would have been drafted if I didn't go. By that time I had developed an interest in languages. I really got into Spanish and did a lot of reading. The wrestling coach at Colorado State College of Education, in Greeley, CO, offered me a work-study scholarship. I worked on buildings and grounds and made the wrestling team, winning about half my matches. After receiving a degree in education and a teaching certificate, I got my first job teaching social studies at Oak Creek High School. *(Continued in Chapter Nine)*

Dulcinea Sandoval Olivas

(An oral history continued from Chapter Three)

In 1951, we moved to Brighton, CO, looking for a better job for my husband. At first we lived in a little house (formerly a chicken house) my oldest brother Eusebio had on his small farm on the south edge of town. George found work at the oil foundry in Derby, now known as Commerce City, on the northern edge of Denver. When we could afford it, we rented a house there so George would be closer to his work. He eventually got a job at nearby Rocky Mountain Arsenal where he helped destroy toxic and chemical weapons. After he retired 33 years later, he worked at Lowry Air Force Base for several years. Now 82 and fully retired, he devotes himself to maintaining our house and yard and tinkering with his cars. He has a beautiful red pickup that he totally rebuilt. It is the envy of every car enthusiast.

Dulcinea and George Olivas at their home in Commerce City, CO.

As time passed, we bought the house we rented and upgraded it many times, so that it is now comfortable and well kept. We had 10 children: Georgia, Edward (who died at the age of six months), Fred, Maxine, Octaviano, George, Teodorita, Robert, Morris and Bobby. They all live in Colorado and have good jobs and nice homes. Teodorita and Morris went to college. All of them have a good work ethic and I am proud of all of them. George and I tried to set a good example for them, to instill in them the values of the people of Terromote and Manuelitas.

I did not know my older brothers well, but I was close to Alfonso and Tavianito. Alfonso died in 1970 when he was hit by a train while working for the Union Pacific Railroad in Wyoming. Tavianito and Ben went to Kansas City after the war and lived there most of their lives. Ben married a woman from Texas named Tomasa; Tavianito, a woman from Mexico named Eleanor. Ben and Tomasa had no children, but Tavianito and Eleanor had five: Lisabet, Tony, Manuel, Irene, and Edward, now a prominent fashion and commercial photographer with an office in Springfield, IL. Tavianito died in 1999. When Ben got Alzheimer's, I brought him to Commerce City and had him admitted to The Rose Care Nursing Center. I visited him often. Sometimes he was very lucid and sometimes lost in a fog. He died in 2006.

Anthony Raymond Alle

(1937-)
(An oral history: 2006)
[Son of Sam Alle and Pablita Sandoval.]

I was born in Carbon County Memorial Hospital in Rawlins, WY., on Oct. 25, 1937, the youngest child of Sam and Pablita Alle, Sara being the eldest, then David, Virginia, and Emma. There were two others before me, Lita and Michael, both of whom died. We lived in Wamsutter, then a tiny community of about 100 people, consisting largely of the crews for two railroad sections and their families, stockyards to hold livestock for shipment, mostly sheep and wild mustangs, and a pumping station for petroleum. The trucking industry was thriving at the time. Wamsutter also served as a sheep-shearing location.

As a boy I cleaned the troughs at the stockyards. Virginia, Emma and I attended a four-room school on railroad property. After I completed the third grade, our family moved to Rawlins, where I began the fourth grade. Four years later, when I was in the eighth grade, my father died, of a heart attack at the age of 58. I feel he died from overwork.

In 1964, when I was 25, my mother, Pablita, died; she was 62. My mother was strict in her religion; she saw to it that all her children were baptized. When you live with someone of a different culture and religion—my father became a Catholic but not a practicing one—it was difficult, but she did the best she could. Both made many friends and were always proud of their family. If you were in trouble, she would even cosign for you. We were very close to Angelica and Tony Lovato and considered their children cousins. They lived in Rock Springs. We would ride the Union Pacific passenger train to visit them. Their home was always open to us.

Anthony R. Alle

Sara, a high school and beauty school graduate, married Floyd Fillin, whose father was the village blacksmith in Ft. Bridger, 98 miles from the Utah border. They had two daughters, Dina and Jennifer, and their grandchildren live in the Phoenix area. She had her own beauty shop and now, in retirement, assists the priests in the area. She is a strong fundraiser, a major driving force in keeping St. Helen's alive and in good standing financially. Among the many roles she fills in her church, serving as a Communion minister has been the most enjoyable and rewarding.

David did not finish high school but later got his GED while in military service. As a teenager he was quite a wrangler, capturing wild horses. In payment, he received part of the herd. He became a professional soldier, rising to master sergeant in the Special Forces. He fought in Korea and Vietnam, winning the Silver Star, two purple hearts, the Bronze Star and several commendations for meritorious service. He was also stationed in Australia, Laos and in Thailand, where he died (of a massive heart attack) when he was in his early 40s. He married a Japanese woman named Masako and they had two daughters, Deedee and Eva, an account executive for Abacus, a computer company. Masako and Deedee live in Fayetteville, N.C., Eva near Atlanta.

Neither Virginia nor Emma graduated from high school but got their GED certificate later. Virginia, twice married, lived in California. From her first husband, Ted Clark, she had two children, Ted Clark Jr., and Sammy, who died. From her second husband, Leroy Davis, she also had two children, Lucille Davis and Howard Davis. She died in California when she was in her 50s. Staying in Wyoming, Emma first married Jimmy Baca and they had four children, Theresa, Albert, Ramona and James Baca; in second marriage, to Fred Rendón, there was only one child, Giana Rendón. Now 71, Emma lives in Casper with Giana.

In Wamsutter, we lived at the foot of the trail to the mountains. My father frequently brought home strangers who needed a meal, a place to stay or a job. He outfitted shepherds and other workers with a bedroll, clothing, perhaps a rifle, food–whatever they needed–trusting them to pay him once they began drawing a wage. He bought and sold animal hides, wild horses and sheep, and all manner of used goods. He knew all the sheep and cattle ranchers and they told him when they needed workers. He had similar contacts on the railroad.

During the Great Depression and dust bowl days of the 1930s when my uncles could hardly survive on their small dry-land farms in New Mexico, my father found temporary or permanent jobs for them in Wyoming. There I met uncles Geraldo Martinez, Alfonso Sandoval, Conrado Aragon and their families. Others had come before, when I was too young to remember. Uncles Octaviano and Ben were in the Army, but I later met Uncle Eusebio in Colorado and Herman in New Mexico. My father also helped many others. His niche in life was to be a good family man, a friend and a good provider. In achieving that, he taught me a core belief, "There are no strangers in the world, only friends you have not met."

If I had listened to some of my advisers, I would never have gone to college. They asked: "How about vocational school?" But you can dream and dreams do come true. When I graduated from high school, the commencement speaker was Mauricio Medina, the salutatorian of our class. One of my best friends, he was my roommate at Carroll College before entering the seminary to become a priest. When I married, he was in my wedding. Later as an ordained priest, he presided over the wedding of our daughter Paula.

Thirty-five years after my high school graduation, I was selected commencement speaker for the class of 1991. It was an emotional occasion to enter the gymnasium (which I helped build as a construction laborer) with my nephew, Emma's grandson, one of the graduates. Others were the sons and daughters of my childhood friends. The superintendent of schools, a young coach when I played football on the starting defensive team for Rawlins High School, welcomed me home.

Alle as a realtor.

I dedicated the commencement speech to my parents and to all those who had made a difference in my life. I titled it, "You are smarter than you think," as my Mom and Dad always used to tell me. I had many role models in my life, but I also used Moises Sandoval and his brothers as models because they were the trailblazers in our family and enjoyed success in their respective careers. One of my most cherished photos is with all the brothers and sister Lucy, except Frankie, the youngest son, not yet born. I would come to visit and stay for months, sleeping in the basement, joining in the family rosary. Moises and cousin Tony were the elders of our group and pioneered in the pursuit of college degrees. Carmel and I would sell the *Grit* newspaper; he had an entrepreneurial spirit, like the Lebanese. He and I attended a summer session at Colorado State in Greeley. I saw his knowledge of educational administration and the importance of personal growth and commitment. He was married to Neva Meginley, a pillar of strength who loved and respected his family.

I also admired my cousin Arsenio, a Spanish scholar whose footsteps I followed to the University of New Mexico, where one of his professors, Dr. Ruben Cobos, was also one of my favorites. My Cousin Ray followed the lead of his brothers and, from all reports, was also a fine instructor. I enjoyed his sense of humor.

When Jay (Eusebio Jr.) was in graduate school at the University of Wyoming, one of his professors, Dr. Don Hawley, was a close friend and former professor of mine. The first time I heard, *De Colores*, I heard it from Jay and asked why they sang such a simple song. "Primo, we'll talk about it later," he replied. Years later, I too became a very active Cursillista and I apologized to him. I was very upset when he died at the age of 27. We came from Illinois to Brighton to pay our final respects. What an athlete he was, so handsome and intelligent and an outstanding educator despite his youth.

For a long time I stayed in touch with my prima Lucy, a dynamic, most articulate person who could hold her own with her clan. Elivinio, *el sacamuelas* (dentist), and I developed a strong bond. He was my mother's godson, with exemplary personal and professional achievements. When I started my own family, I was too busy pursuing my career to stay in touch, but my love, respect and admiration remained alive in my heart and mind.

I dreamed of becoming a lawyer, but my father talked me out of going to law school. "Why would you want to work with crooks every day?" Such was his perception of lawyers. So I went into education, graduating from Carroll College in Montana, from the University of Wyoming graduate school, the University of New Mexico's National Defense Education Act's Graduate Certificate Program in linguistics and from Thunderbird, the American Graduate School of International Management, in Glendale, AZ, with a master's degree in international management/business/marketing.

I worked in Alaska, California and in Illinois, where I taught business administration, international management, Spanish and English as a second language at Illinois Central College in Peoria for 27 years, retiring as a full professor. I was twice recognized as educator of the year, the only professor in the history of my college to be so honored in different academic areas. I also became a licensed realtor in the state of Illinois and a certified real estate instructor.

In Carroll College, I met my future wife, the former Martha Stowe, a nursing graduate from that school. We have three children. Paula, the eldest has a nursing degree and a master's in business administration and is a realtor in Scottsdale and Phoenix. An outstanding distance runner, she will be inducted into the Peoria hall of fame. She and her husband Ron Henry have two sons, Jackson David and Michael Richard, ages three and five. Our son Michael is a mechanical engineer with a master's in business administration and works in global purchasing for Caterpillar Tractor in Raleigh, NC. Martha Rose, our other daughter, graduated from Illinois Central College and from Life Path, a top school of massage therapy, and now does that kind of work in Phoenix. She has a daughter, Lilly Rose.

When I was young I did not realize that I was half Lebanese. Now I speak some Arabic, having studied it with some friends and learned from former students and from my involvement with the Lebanese community in Peoria. I can greet you and engage in basic dialogue. When people ask me who I am, I say, "I am Anthony R. Alle de Sandoval." Peoria had many prominent Lebanese, including the U.S. congressman who presided over Bill Clinton's impeachment, the former mayor for whom I worked in real estate brokerage after my retirement, judges, doctors, lawyers, a state senator and the biggest commercial developer and many businessmen. I knew the majority on a first-name basis–Lakis, Haddad, Barrack, Malouf, Seman, McMurry, Couri, Marron, Ghantous, Joseph, Lahood, Sharraf, Basawi, Banjak and many others. Many of their children were my college students. I became acquainted with my father's roots and heritage through my friendship with those Lebanese families and with the students from the Middle East at my college. Twenty-two came from Tyre, five of them brothers from one family. Besides those from Lebanon, I also taught young men from the Saudi Arabian Peninsula, Kuwait and Iran.

In the 27 years I taught international management at Illinois Central College, I was surrogate father for 150 students, all non-Christians from Lebanon. When they came and sought me out, I said to myself, "My Dad is not here, but I am in a position to guide these boys." My wife Martha and I opened our home to them. All did well after graduation, one becoming a vice president in Dubai, the United Arab Emirates, others gaining prominence in business and in the professions. One owns a deli and a Middle Eastern restaurant in Phoenix.

During a Cursillo right after 9/11, I shared the story of these wonderful boys. I said: "The values I have did not come from a priest, or the Church or the Catholic college I attended. I got them from my father, who was from Lebanon, and from my mother, who was from good stock in New Mexico and sang in the church." I helped to start the Hispanic church in Peoria; it is going strong now.

Leo de Herrera, whose dad worked alongside mine on the railroad, is the city attorney in Rawlins and his brother was U.S. marshal for the state of Wyoming. My cousin Leopoldo Aragon, once also a railroader in Tipton, became a successful upholsterer in Casper. These and many others, *pura raza*, accepted the responsibility of bettering their lives and did very well.

I did not meet my grandfather Octaviano Sandoval, but he must have been a bright guy. Intelligent people do not have to be academically trained. Some from the rancho may not have gone to the sixth grade, but they had the education of life. That is why I admired the family of Eusebio and Amada Sandoval so much, but other cousins were phenomenal too. I have precious memories of Uncle Geraldo Martinez, Tia Ignacita, my godmother–she knew more about the Church than we would ever know–and Uncle Conrado, my godfather for confirmation. I visited my Grandma Teodorita when she lived in Greeley, CO, with Tia Ignacita, bringing her a box of Bull Durham tobacco and a pint of whisky–for medicinal purposes. I also appreciated the Olivas family; my uncle George was exceptional.

My home when I was growing up was adequate, but not a place to socialize, to bring a friend, because I never knew what stranger would be at our table. But it had a big pantry with stacks of five-gallon tins of soy sauce, cases of spaghetti and macaroni, big bottles of olive oil and olives, tins of honey, sacks of flour, cases of canned goods and plenty of mutton and venison in the freezers. All of us children slept in the same bed. When I talk about those days, my own children say: "Dad you really lived in primitive times." I respond that if I did I did not know it. I consider myself very fortunate to have come from such a diverse family. All did the best they could.

Quedo muy agradecido de toda la familia. Todos contribuyeron en una manera u otra. Es un orgullo y placer de haber compartido unos detalles del desarrollo de nuestra vida. Hay muchos capítulos que no he discutido. Sin embargo, felicitaciones y que sigan disfrutando su vida.

(I am grateful to all the family. All contributed in one way or another. I am proud and pleased to contribute a few details of the development of our life. There are many chapters I have not discussed. Nevertheless, congratulations and (the hope) all will continue to enjoy their lives.)

Dr. Antonio Sandoval

Part memoir, part oral history
(Continued from Chapter Five)

In 1944 our family moved to Brighton, CO and the first girl in our family after seven boys was born. Up until that year every baby our mother had was a boy. I was in 7th grade. The classes at Brighton Junior High School were divided into A, B and C groups. The students with higher ability were placed in the A group and in-coming Hispanics were automatically placed in the C group. So that's where I was placed, but after a few weeks in the C group I was transferred to the A group.

At Brighton Junior High I didn't participate in sports, but I did participate in school plays. In eighth grade our class performed Charles Dickens' Christmas Carol. Because I was the smallest student in the class I had the part of Tiny Tim. I also loved to present declamations and memorize poetry. My cousin José Perea remembers that while we were studying The Highwayman by Alfred Noyes, the teacher asked us to memorize one verse. On the way home that day, I suggested to José that we memorize the entire poem. At the next class, the teacher, Mrs. Harris, asked who had memorized the verse. The students responded with dead silence. Then I raised my hand, stood up, and recited all 17 verses, to the amazement of Mrs. Harris. After I sat down José Perea raised his hand, stood up, and was three-quarters of the way through the poem when Mrs. Harris said, "All right, all right, you memorized the whole poem too. Sit down."

In spite of what I did in Mrs. Harris' English class I still got a failing grade. At the end of the year we had to turn in our last book report. I had read a book that was a collection of short stories. Earlier in the year I had written a report on one of the stories from that book. Shortly before 8th grade graduation Mrs. Harris told me, "You are getting an "F" in my class because you violated the rules. You reported on the same book twice." I tried to explain to her that I had only read one of the stories earlier in the year, but she wouldn't budge. After the graduation ceremony I was shocked to see an "F" in English on my report card. I ran home ahead of Mom, I entered the house through a window, found a pen that matched the color of ink on my "F." I changed my "F" to an "A," quickly got out of the house the way I went in and waited for Mom to arrive so I could present my report card to her. My crime was never discovered and I didn't confess it until several years later.

At Brighton Junior High School I learned to love science. The science teacher, Mrs. Klaus, had a microscope and would let us look at a variety of things. It was at that time that my love of reading also developed. I sold the *Grit* newspaper, a national weekly, door-to-door. This newspaper had serial stories that captivated me. I looked forward to reading the next installment every week. At this time, my older brother, Moises, was also into reading, more so than I was. He loved to read Zane Grey novels. I remember nights when Dad would say, "Ok, lights out." Moises would continue reading under the blankets with a flashlight.

When I started High School in Brighton in 1946, I couldn't decide what kind of diploma I wanted; so I was classified as a student pursuing a general education diploma. Brighton High offered college preparatory, commercial, agricultural, home economics (for girls) and general diplomas. In the general diploma curriculum, one could take any class one chose and only one English class and general math were required.

But by graduation day, I lacked only a history class to have a college preparatory diploma. My favorite subjects were chemistry, physics and geometry. My chemistry teacher was Mr. White. He was a no-nonsense type of teacher who seldom smiled, but was fair and knew his chemistry. I memorized the names and properties of elements in the periodic table including atomic numbers and atomic weights. One summer I was working for the Western Foods Pickle Dock, which at the time was run by two college students from Colorado State University. One day they said, "We can't work today. We forgot our handbooks and we can't calculate the amount of salt we need for brine tanks for the pickling process." I asked them, "What do you need to know." They said they needed the atomic weights of sodium and chlorine. I gave them the weights to several decimal figures and the work went on.

During high school I lettered in track. I ran the mile, but I really didn't have time for other activities. On some weekends we worked at nearby farms or set pins at the Brighton bowling alley at night. I didn't go to the prom dances. I attended the prom dinners with other boys who didn't have dates.

Before graduating from high school, I became fascinated by radios. I traded a radio for a book that explained how radios worked. After graduation I wanted to go to the Coyne School of Electronics in Chicago. I never got there because Mom wanted me to go to a Catholic college or university. She hoped that by going to a Catholic College I might decide to become a priest. One day she asked me to promise her that I would go to a Catholic College for at least one year. "After one year, you can do whatever you want to do," she said. I promised her that I would and then Mom and I went to Regis College to talk to an academic counselor. That fall I enrolled at Regis College.

I went with the intention of going only one year. However, once I started I decided to go all four years because I really loved chemistry. Regis had a very good program in chemistry. It gave entering students the American Chemical Association exam usually given to chemistry students after they have completed one year. When I took that exam—although they never told me then—I scored in the 98th percentile. Then after I completed a year of chemistry the following summer, the priest professor was telling us how much we had improved and then he looked at me and said, "You are the one who improved the least. You scored a 98 when you began college and you only improved one percentage point, to 99. That is when I decided to go the whole way. There were seven chemistry majors—the enrollment at Regis was only around 450 students—and six went on to get PhDs. But we worked together. I received my PhD at Kansas State University.

I was in an area where there were few Hispanics. When I was a professor at the University of Missouri at Kansas City, I joined the Society for the Advancement of Chicanos and Native Americans in science and at that time there were only six Chicanos with PhD's. I was probably the first Hispanic who got a PhD. in chemistry in the state of Colorado, though I have never checked that out. And one of the reasons is that the curriculum is more difficult because you have to take a lot of math. It was a real challenge, and I was in a very competitive group. In my four years at Regis I went to only one basketball game and Regis had a national reputation at the time.

It was also difficult because I worked from 35 to 40 hours a week as an orderly, most of the time at St. Joseph Hospital but also at St. Anthony Hospital around my junior year. I remember when I started at Regis seeing a sign on the bulletin board at the college that St. Joseph was looking for orderlies. I needed a job and I applied even though I did not know what an orderly was. I interviewed with a Sister Agnes and she asked me, "Do you think you would like to be an orderly?" I said: "Oh, yes, I sure would love to be an orderly." And she said: "Ok, you're hired." I went home and looked up in a dictionary what an orderly was. I always worked there on the 4-11 p. m. shift. I never worked weekends; it was my time to study.

The advantage of working at the hospital was that they provided us with a meal at the end of the shift, sometimes when we distributed the trays if somebody did not want their food or went home. The other thing is that I really loved the work. I remember saying this is a job that if my replacement doesn't show up I will take that shift too. It was helping people and I think I had that orientation at that time. That became my way of learning.

As a professional I also was very successful because in seven years I became a full professor. Usually you start as assistant professor, then associate professor and then professor. I also did research at Colorado University for two summers, 1964 and 1965, with a Dr. Melvin Hanna. The ultimate end was cancer research, but really what we were studying was the binding of aromatic compounds to (another compound) that resembles the DNA. Then I also did some research at the Salk Institute with a Dr. Leslie Orgel in La Joya, CA, a very interesting environment. While I was there several people won the Nobel Prize and we had a great celebration in the courtyard. Anyway, it was the cutting edge of research, and I had the opportunity to work there for a year. *(Continued in Chapter Ten)*

Dr. José Perea

(An oral history)
(Continued from Chapter Five)

When I started school in Henderson, CO, I was six years old and did not know a word of English. No other student spoke Spanish; I was a very quiet kid, sitting in the back of the room. One day, however, the teacher opened a little book and, showing some pictures at the same time, began reading a story about a kangaroo. I remember it to this day:

"Said the kind kangaroo, 'Oh, what shall I do? If I had a cradle, I would rock it. But I think, after all, since my baby is so small, I will carry him in my pocket.'" I laughed so hard the teacher noticed. She walked to my desk and said, "You liked that story. What did you like about it?" I replied in halting words:

"The kangaroo in the pocket." The teacher realized then that I did not know English. She had me stay in for part of every recess so she could teach me. Since Papa Enrique had taught Jake and me to read a little in Spanish, it really was not hard to learn English. But we did not stay long in Henderson. Martin was fired from the job on the vegetable farm because he was a thief. He had me help him dig potatoes at night; I guess he just had to have the potatoes. He got a job at a farm that raised chickens but was fired there too. He used to come home at night with two chickens. We came back to the Trujillo farm in Terromote, but the one-room school there had been closed and I had to go to Rociada for the second grade.

The teacher gave us a little talk about what we were going to learn. She held up a book and said: "I am going to teach you to read this book." When she finished I was in tears. She asked: "Why are you crying?"

"I have already read that book."

"So you think you are so smart. Read me this page," (the introduction to the third-grade math book). I did and she told me, "Go and sit with the third graders." Antonio (Sandoval) was in the same class. The next year, Martin moved to Las Vegas, renting a place from my uncle Lolo (Perea). I started the fourth grade in Las Vegas. We used to play marbles and baseball, me and the other kids in the neighborhood. One day I got a beating after getting home from catechism. The nuns had changed the class from Monday to Tuesday and Martin thought I had been playing. He claimed I had been seen playing by the courthouse, which was not true. One Saturday, a friend and I went to see a cowboy movie at the Kiva theater and my friend said: "Let's see the beginning again, but we ended up seeing the whole movie. I was afraid to go home because when we got out it was dark. When I got home Martin beat me and said, "I am going to write a letter to your grandfather Juan to come for you. When my Tio Maque came a few days later, Martin said: "You came to us with only the clothes you were wearing and that is how you are going to leave. I had a mechanical pencil I had found and he took that too.

My Tio and I got a ride on a truck that had brought mine props to Las Vegas. It let us out by San Ysidro. We walked through the woods–it was already dark–and all the way home I heard the coyotes yelping. I was then nine years old. The next morning my Grandfather Juan said: "Let Peggy show him the ranch." He had married a widow named Alice from Arkansas with four daughters. Most recently, the family had lived in Guadalupita, NM, the husband dying there. Peggy took me to see the goats. She showed me the dog, named Safao, and took me all over the ranch. About 3 p. m, I heard some banging and asked Peggy what that was. She replied: "Oh, those are my sisters coming home from school." When they got there, she introduced me to Rita Mae and Bessie Belle. Tio Maque had shacked up with the oldest, Viola Fabiola. All of the girls spoke Spanish but not their mother. Since my grandfather did not speak English, they used a lot of sign language. The one-room school nearby was also called Terromote School (like the one in Peñasco). I finished the fourth grade there. On my first day at the school, I was embarrassed by one of the Quintana girls. She passed me a note asking, "Will you be my boyfriend?" I stayed there one year.

A lot of things happened. One day Alice, who used to chew tobacco, hit me with a rolling pin just as my grandfather was walking in the house. He got angry and yelled at her. Then he said: "This old lady will not get after you again." Then he shared a *piloncillo* with me, saying: "This is for you and me only; let the gringas eat shit. Tomorrow I will talk to my compadre to see if you can live there." I went to live with Grandpa Enrique, Grandma Josefita and (cousin) Fefa, who had lived with them. Tia Juanita, Uncle Juan Perea's widow, and Tia Alcarita, my grandfather's sister, also lived at the ranch. I stayed until the end of the next year, 1942 or 1943, when Grandpa sold the ranch because my grandmother was very sick. He wanted to move to town so that they would be close to the hospital. I do not know what illness she had, but she became very mean. She used to hit us with a strap.

José and Stella Perea in 2004.

My grandfather sold a Jersey cow with a calf for $125 and the ranch for $600. The buyer, Adolfo Chavez, was also interested in buying a high-powered rifle that my Tia Juanita had. We were in the kitchen discussing terms. She wanted $80 and would not budge on the price. Chavez offered $50, then $60, and then $70, but she remained firm. He said, "You have to come down too." Finally, she said, "Ok, I will come down to $77." They tried to get her down to $75 but she said no and he finally bought it for $77, with six boxes of ammunition.

It was a beautiful rifle, hardly ever used, belonging to my uncle Juan, who died of tuberculosis in 1939. My uncle Eusebio borrowed the gun sometimes to hunt and once shot three deer. He and Papa Enrique brought them down from the hills in a wagon to his house. They skinned them there and Eusebio gave us some of the meat, including the head of one. My grandfather cooked it. Another time, shortly before we moved to town, we went to Uncle Eusebio's house and bought a kid goat for 50 cents.

Grandfather Perea gave Uncle Lolo and Uncle Melecio $100 each and bought a small house near Uncle Lolo's in Las Vegas for $400. He took his horses and wagon to town and used them to help a man in nearby Montezuma make adobe (mud) bricks to build houses.

In Las Vegas, Fefa, who had a job at a grocery store, took me to the movies, giving me the money for admission. One time we met her boyfriend, who walked her home while I followed some distance behind. I went through the fifth, sixth and seventh grades in Las Vegas, passing the 7th grade "on condition" because the teacher and I did not get along. Then Grandma Josefita and Grandpa Enrique sent Jake and me to live with our father in Brighton. "I am tired of taking care of children," Grandma said. I do not know how old she was then but she must have been in her 70s, for they had celebrated their 50th wedding anniversary. Jake and I went to Colorado by bus, each with 50 cents given to us by Uncle Lolo.

Papa Pedro was working for the railroad and was married to a woman named Leonor (I never knew her last name). They lived in half of a house owned by her parents. I stayed there only a month or two, just for the summer. Jake stayed a little longer. Then I went to live with Tia Quirina Aragon, also living in Brighton. She said: "Why don't you come here; Arturo (her only son) needs a playmate." I lived there one year, completing the eighth grade with very good grades. Tony and I were classmates again and we were inseparable. He was always trying to blow the top off the tests.

Arturo, however, was hard to tolerate. My uncle Filadelfio Aragon, who worked at Fitzsimons Army Hospital in Aurora, would bring comic books, unavailable to the public during World War II. But Arturo took them all and would not let me see them. When I wanted something from the table, like the sugar, he would not let me have it, and my aunt and uncle would not make him pass it to me. My aunt could not understand how I could be so friendly with Tony and not get along with Arturo. During the summer I worked in the fields and earned enough to buy myself a second-hand bike for $17. Arturo had a brand new one, but he took my bike and ran it into a fence, bending the wheel. I retaliated by letting the air out of his tires. My aunt and uncle then decided I had to leave. My uncle was almost crying when he told me I had to go.

I got on the bus and went back to Las Vegas. Grandma Josefita had died by then and my grandfather had married Francisquita, another little old lady. I stayed with them for a year, when she decided she did not want me around. She said she did not want to be raising children. It was summer and I was only 13. "You have to go," my grandfather said. "I suggest you go to Colorado. There is much work there. We do not have the money to pay your fare, but if you enlist *("te renganchas")* they will pay your fare and give you a place to live." He told me to go to the Labor Department to apply.

But Grandpa first taught me some survival skills. "I am going to teach you how to make a *mochila* (bedroll)," he said. He took a piece of canvas and a blanket, told me to get a shirt, a pair of trousers, socks and a toothbrush. Then he taught me how to fold them into a bedroll. At the Labor Department office, where I went with a friend, we enlisted and received a train ticket. At the train station we were told we were leaving right away, going to Rocky Ford, CO. I never thought of going home for my *mochila*. There were 14 of us from Las Vegas, delinquents 14, 15, 16 and only one 18; I was the youngest.

Upon arriving, we were met by guy named Nava, a Mexican labor contractor who had done well in Colorado. He took us to a little old house in the middle of a field with only two rooms, only one bed and no mattress. Some of our group went to a nearby labor camp to steal blankets from houses and cars. They stole everything they could find and came back with armloads, two gallons of wine, several loaves of bread and two pounds of baloney. We hit the wine and ate the food. The next day a truck came for us at 4 a. m. and took us to an onion field. We got short-handled hoes, the cost to be taken out of our pay, and set to work hoeing and thinning the plants. At the end of the day we could not stand up. Other workers had to push us up on the truck. My companions went out to buy food and came back with more baloney, bread and another two gallons of wine. That is how it went the first week, at the end of which, having earned enough for the fare back to Las Vegas, most of them left.

Four days later the rest, except for George Coca and me, went home too. I had no place to go and the police in Las Vegas wanted George for breaking into a store. Alongside us worked a family with a little girl 12 years old who often helped me because I was very slow. She would do her row and part of mine. Her parents allowed George and me to live in the cellar of their house. George, however, soon quit and, because he was much older, forced me to lend him some of my money. One day, because he refused to pay me back, we had a knockdown fight in the yard, rolling on the ground like dogs. The man came out, separated us and told George to get out of his house. The family then invited me to live upstairs with them. I slept in the same room with the girl, she in the top bunk and I in the lower one. The family did not take a penny for food or rent; I was getting $25 a week and saved most of it, staying with them all summer and into the fall. Then, with $125 in my pocket, I returned to Las Vegas. After the season ended, the family, from Colorado, visited me in Las Vegas.

My uncle Lolo was then in a sanatorium in San Antonio being treated for tuberculosis. Since I could no longer live with my grandfather, Uncle Lolo's, wife, Tia Julia, let me stay with her. She could hardly afford it because she was getting child support from the Welfare Department but thought they might help me too, if I asked. When I walked into the Welfare Department and told them I wanted to apply for welfare, they almost rolled in the aisles with laughter. Finally, a woman heard my story and asked, "Isn't there anyone you can live with?" I told them my aunt Julia might take me in.

"Let's go talk to her," the woman said. The official told Tia Julia they could provide $15 a month and food stamps for my support. I lived with her for a year. I gave her my $125 and she bought me five pairs of pants, five shirts, five pairs of socks and five pairs of underwear. She had me change to clean clothes every day. It was the cleanest I had ever been.

When the school year ended, I decided to return to Colorado. I was packing my *mochila*, determined not to forget it this time, when Feliciano Armijo, the personnel director at the State Mental Hospital and a relative of my uncle Lolo's, walked in and said: "I may be able to help you. I may be able to get you on as an attendant." Telling me I would have a room and meals, he suggested: "Let's fill out an application. Then we will go see Apolonio Duran (the director)." Finding I was only 15, he said. "You have to say you are 17."

Instead of going to Colorado I went to work at the State Hospital, 10 hours a day six days a week and received $55 a month plus my room and board for almost three years. During that time, I went to high school, but did not finish. With my savings, I had bought a used 1938 Plymouth. One night in February of 1950, five of us, including my cousin Henry Perea, went to Santa Fe to see West Las Vegas play in the district basketball tournament, which we won. We spent the night in a hotel and started home about 9:30 the next morning. But about 10 miles out of Santa Fe while going down a steep hill, all of a sudden a wheel slipped off the pavement on the narrow two-lane road. As I tried to get back on the pavement, the right front wheel came off and the car rolled over. One of the girls broke a leg and Henry, thrown from the car, was killed. I was mentally crushed. Of all the people in the car, he was the best person. Both of us worked at the State Hospital and took our vacations together. I asked, "Why wasn't I killed instead?" I lost all interest in school and in March joined the army. Since I was still 17, my uncle Melecio had to sign for me. I became 18 in April.

I finished my three-year enlistment in March of 1953, returning to Las Vegas with a friend from the Army, William Duran, from Monte Aplanado. Grandfather Perea's second wife had died by then and we lived with him. We often sat on the front porch drinking beer and watching the girls go by. One of them, Stella Gonzales, passed by often on her way to a little neighborhood store. We met and liked each other. Like me, she was an orphan, living with her aunt. When I asked her permission to date her niece, she told me I was not good enough. Reluctantly, she allowed us to date only between 5-6 p. m. every Friday. Soon, however, we were ignoring the limits and her attitude got worse and worse. So we decided to get married. We started going together in May and got married on Dec. 5, 1953. The aunt disowned Stella, saying: "She is not my daughter."

By then I had started college on the GI Bill at New Mexico Highlands University, having earned my GED (General Education Diploma) while in the army at White Sands. We rented a little apartment for $10 a month; it was quite run down, but we didn't have much money. Stella, then in the 11th grade, quit school, got her GED and worked at a bank, starting as a teller, working her way up into book-keeping, then machine posting and finally, in 1959, into being in charge of all bookkeeping. I started out in pre-med because I had been a medic in Korea and had served out my enlistment working in the lab. I thought I would go to medical school but when I went deeply in debt I became discouraged and went into teaching instead. By the time I graduated we had two children, Lorraine and Ricky.

I taught the fourth, fifth and sixth grades for nine years in Vaughn, NM, from 1956 to 1965. During that time I continued my studies at Highlands and in 1960 received a master's degree in educational administration. Thinking that with one more year of graduate work I could get a job as a principal, I enrolled in a program at the University of New Mexico taught by Tom Wiley, a colorful character who had done it all: teacher, principal, superintendent, state superintendent of public instruction and now college professor. Telling myself I had to go for straight A's I was sitting at the front of the classroom and quickly raised my hand when he asked one day:

"What does it take to become a superintendent in the state of New Mexico?"

As I started to enumerate all the administrative credentials needed, he interrupted: "You are dead wrong. It takes three board members out of five."

It so happened that Vaughn was looking for a superintendent. A lawyer had been running the district for six months for $3,000 a month. I thought to myself, I can swing three members out of five. I had sold World Book Encyclopedias door-to-door the summer before and I had learned how to sell, how to influence people and close the deal. However, the board had already decided on a guy named Eloy Blea. When I called they agreed to give me only a brief courtesy interview, but I insisted they ask me every question on the full-fledged interview. The lawyer asked me all the questions and I told them: "You want a superintendent who understands the people." The other candidates were from Texas and Tierra Amarilla. I won the job by a 3-2 vote.

During the four years I was superintendent, I wrote the educational specifications for a new school, passed a bond issue, and gave the specifications to an architect who designed the school. When it was completed, I invited Richard Holman, chairman of the Educational Administration Department at the University of New Mexico to come to the dedication and he brought Dr. Richard Tonigan, professor in charge of facilities planning. As I was driving them back to the plane, Tonigan asked me. "How would you like to work for a doctorate? What would it take?"

"Enough to survive," I replied. I received a research assistantship that paid me $200 a month and committed myself to complete my PhD. in two years. Stella, working at the local bank, transferred to a branch in Corrales (near Albuquerque). I received no financial aid. I started in 1969 and defended my dissertation in 1971. I worked one year at New Mexico State University in Las Cruces as an assistant professor in educational administration and then became dean of general studies at the Auraria campus of Denver Community College. *(Continued in Chapter Eight)*

Irene Sandoval
(1945-)
(An oral history: 2005)

I am the oldest of the 12 children—four sisters and eight brothers—born in 1945 in Las Vegas, in a house still standing on 321 Tecolote Street. My parents, Alfonso and Dora Sandoval, had married when she was 16 and he was 19. My father was not there when I was born; he was in the army undergoing basic training. But he came home soon afterward because the war ended. He felt left out because his brothers—Benjamin, Octaviano Jr. and Herman and his brothers-in-law Geraldo Martinez and George Olivas—had all gone to war. However, when he died in 1970, he was honored with a military funeral complete with a 21-gun salute.

For some time after my father came home we lived with Grandfather Octaviano in Terromote. He came out to greet us. He stretched his arms out to me and carried me into the house. The women were always cooking and canning. My grandma Teodorita was always making tortillas. I followed my dad to the orchard, to the cornfields. I used to climb a fruit tree in front of the house. There was a dam behind grandpa's house and my father went swimming there. He would dive into the deepest part, taking a long time to come back up. After that we lived in a little cabin, just two rooms, where my uncle Herman lives now, alongside Highway 94. My uncle Herman and my father kept a herd of sheep and goats and sold wood to town residents.

Then we went to live with our maternal grandfather, Pablo Lucero, who came for us in a wagon pulled by horses. It was cold and my dad wrapped me in a quilt. I remember the sound of the horses and of the wheels as my grandpa pulled on the wooden brake to slow the wagon going down a hill. It was nearly dark when we arrived at his house. We lived there until I was almost six. I still remember the day we left for Las Vegas. My father had a blue Model-A car, the kind you had to crank to start. He put us in it—my Mom, then pregnant with Ernesto, my brother Alfonso, Katie and I—and we drove to Las Vegas. I was six years old when I started kindergarten and didn't speak a word of English. Fortunately, my teacher spoke Spanish.

We moved a lot following my father's work. At one time we worked for the railroad in Plainview, CO. We lived in a boxcar with no windows, just a sliding door and a small camping stove. When I was nine years old, we lived for a time in Greeley, Colo., where my Tia Ignacita worked as the housekeeper for the parish priest. We lived in my grandma's basement. One day she became sick and my Tia Ignacita called an ambulance to take her to the hospital. When it did not come right away, my grandmother, sitting in a room waiting patiently, said: "Va, y tan apurada que estaba Ignacita." (Gosh! And Ignacita was in such a hurry.) The ambulance finally came. I never saw my grandmother alive again; she died at the hospital.

From Greeley we moved back to Las Vegas where my dad worked for the New Mexico State Mental Hospital, but he got laid off because he voted for the wrong party—everything was too political there. Not being one to let his family suffer, he went to Wyoming where he found work as a shepherd and then, when my Uncle Conrado and my uncle Sam Alle helped him find a

Irene Sandoval in 2005.

job as a track laborer with the Union Pacific, we moved there. We lived in Tipton, near the red desert, in the middle of nowhere, 50 miles from Rock Springs and 50 miles from Rawlins. Only five families lived there, one that of Tio Conrado and Tia Juanita. Our house had only three rooms, a kitchen in the middle and two bedrooms, one a little larger than the other. We went to a one-room school for grades one through eighth, with 10 or 12 students, among them my brothers Alfonso Jr. and Ernie, my sister Katie and me and our cousins Benjamin, Ernesto and Jane Aragon. I was in the fifth grade and did not learn much. To avoid other work, we begged the teacher to read us Huckleberry Finn from beginning to end. She took us to the movies and bought us hamburgers on some weekends. I found a sunny spot on the top shelf of the supply closet, helped myself to the art materials, drew pictures and read all day. Our teacher was fired at the end of the year.

Every time my father got laid off, my mother panicked and we moved back to Las Vegas. She felt secure living near her family, as they helped us out until my father was called back to work. When I was in the eighth grade, the family joined my father again in Wyoming, but I remained in Las Vegas with my mother's older sister, Guadalupe Trujillo, a teacher and my godmother. To go to high school I would have had to live in Rawlins with my Aunt Pablita Alle, whom I did not know well. Since I was very close to Guadalupe, my parents gave me permission to go to high school in Las Vegas. Before starting the 9th grade, however, I met a 17-year-old boy named Tony Rumaldo Montoya and before I knew it I was pregnant. I was only 15 years old. Blaming each other for my pregnancy, Mom and Dad almost filed for divorce. Finally, they sought counsel from a priest and came down for a small wedding. Shortly after, my boyfriend joined the Army reserve and went on active duty while I went to live with his grandparents. I named our son Anthony Dwayne Montoya.

When I was 17 my mother-in-law moved to San Francisco with her second husband and took all of us with her. We were there, in the mid-1960s, during the Vietnam protests, the civil rights movement and the beginning of the drug culture. I remember a song that said, "If you are coming to San Francisco, wear flowers in your hair." It was a wonderful time to be in San Francisco. We did not stay long, returning to Las Vegas.

After a while, however, I found myself alone; my husband abandoned us and went back to San Francisco. I got a job as a waitress and my baby and I lived with my aunt Guadalupe. I thought I would be doomed to a career waiting tables. One day her son, then in college, asked, "How much would it cost to send Irene back to school?" They talked to the principal, Blas Lopez, a cousin of theirs, and he agreed to let me enroll in the 9th grade. But it was humiliating; I had been out three years and my class was graduating that year.

Nevertheless, the freshmen made me feel welcome, asking me to run for cheerleader. But within one month, my husband called saying he had wired the bus fare so I could take the Greyhound bus to San Francisco. I was hesitant at first, but when he talked to my aunt Guadalupe and promised to allow me to attend night classes at Mission High School, I agreed to go. I remember crossing the Golden Gate Bridge with my oldest son, Anthony, then three years old, sitting in my lap. It was almost dark and San Francisco looked so beautiful, all lit up like Christmas, that I fell in love with it.

Soon, however, I learned why my husband and his family invited me back. I had to be the housekeeper, laundress and babysitter for my husband's younger siblings, aged eight, five and four. I wanted to go home to my parents in Wyoming, but I was pregnant again. But during that time I found the nearest public library. I went there and checked out books I read again and again. I remembered what my eighth grade teacher had once told our class: "If you can read you can teach yourself anything." My second child, Valiente Roman was born when I was 19. We moved out of my mother-in-law's house, but I soon found myself alone again. Since I could not depend on my husband, I volunteered to be part of a poverty program that paid for my schooling and childcare. I had been out of school for four years. "Let's see where you are," my teachers said. I could do math only at the fifth grade level, but my reading skill was better than the 11th grade, because of all the reading I had done. So I just brushed up on my math and passed the GED test.

I thought of becoming a nurse, but then my husband decided to come back. But he insisted I quit school and get a job. So I became a telephone operator with Pacific Bell, working there for the next three years. I had to take the bus to work, transferring three times and sometimes the rain drenched me. When I had my third child, Christopher, when I was 25, I quit my job, determined to stay home to care for him. During that time, I also took care of a little girl.

When we first moved to San Francisco, my husband worked as a dishwasher. But one of the times we were separated and lived with his mother, he came one day and said: "I met this guy who said I could join the (labor) union, but they want $10 and I don't have it. I had $10 and gave it to him. He joined, got into construction work and worked five years underground building the Bay Area rapid transit system. During that time he took drugs, but I didn't because I took my role as a mother seriously and I think that saved me. I was trying to give my children the best upbringing.

But my resolve to stay home with my third child did not last long. After three years, I enrolled at the San Francisco School for Health Professions and took a six-month crash course to become a medical assistant. Then I worked three years as medical secretary for Dr. Vicente Vizcaino. My next job was at the University of California Medical School, where I worked ten years, most of the time at San Francisco General Hospital.

In 1986 when our oldest son got married and the second one joined the Navy, both within six months of each other, my marriage ended. I moved back to New Mexico, determined to go to college. I started at New Mexico Highlands when I was 41 years old, graduating five years later with a degree in social work. In one class, one of my classmates was my grandson. I then applied for graduate school and, while waiting to see if I were accepted, took a summer job at the University of San Francisco. The day the letter of acceptance came I was working downtown at 44 Montgomery Street in a building with marble floors, piped in tropical music and gold plated elevators. They gave me a going-away party and that same day I flew to New Mexico. In Las Vegas, my mother-in-law had rented a two-room adobe house for me. I slept that night in my little adobe house, freezing because it had no heat and only candles for light.

I was accepted into the advanced standing program and finished my master's in one year, one of the most difficult in my life. I chose mental health instead of geriatrics because the New Mexico State Mental Hospital is in Las Vegas. I thought this would be a good place to work and live. I would have something to give to my community. I work now as a mental health therapist with the New Mexico Behavioral Health Institute. I deal with outpatients, people from the community who suffer from depression, anxiety and other mental disorders, 84 clients in all.

While I was in college, my son Anthony's marriage ended and he received full custody of his daughter, Athena, then four and a half years old. She came to live with me, blessing me with the daughter I never had. In May of 1994, I suffered the worst tragedy of my life; my second son, Valiente, died in a one-car crash on Martin Luther King Drive in Golden State Park. At his funeral, the priest described him as a rainbow of hope. He had graduated from Riordan Catholic High School, served six years in the Navy and dreamed of becoming a civil rights lawyer. He was 29.

My other two sons live in San Francisco. Anthony is an environmental supervisor with the city and county Department of Public Works. Christopher, 35, works for Lexus in leasing and sales. My former husband, Tony, stayed for 10 years with the union he joined with the $10 I gave him. Then he went to work for the city and county as a foreman in the street repairs department. Now he is vice president of the union I helped him join and a recovering alcoholic, sober for the last 10 years.

I have not had an easy life. Giving birth to my first child at 15, I did not have much of a childhood. Sometimes I think I got cheated out of my adolescence. During my teenage years I was a Mom and I took that very seriously. So I look forward to my retirement in a small adobe house on a quarter of an acre alongside the Pecos River in Villanueva, NM. I look forward to fixing it and spending many happy years there.

[In the summer of 2007, Irene suffered another devastating loss. Her oldest son, Anthony, only 45 years old, died suddenly from a heart attack.]

80 Beyond Terromote

CHAPTER SEVEN

WORKING SMARTS

When cousin Celestino Aragon joined the Army at the age of 17, he failed the IQ test. "It was because I had only been to the fifth grade," he explained. "I didn't know how to do it." Time proved he was sufficiently intelligent. He became a mechanic, an upholsterer, businessman, musician, and a beekeeper. Now in his 70s he can program a satellite dish and fix a computer, installing a new motherboard, a hard-drive and other parts. He became a success by working, always working, as many others from Terromote.

Ask people from there what was the most important thing their parents taught them and they answer, "To work." It was not just working, however, but working smart, or using *mania*, as my father Eusebio put it. Grandfather Perea would cut logs 20 inches in diameter into six-foot lengths and load them on the wagon by rolling them up a ramp using the power of a fulcrum. Leandro Sandoval, a half-brother of Grandpa Octaviano, used the mechanical advantage provided by pulleys to hoist heavy stones for the walls of the family's home. The inhabitants of Terromote were a resourceful people who had many skills, from building their own homes to forging their own tools to thrashing their own beans and peas by stomping the vines with a team of horses. Today, boxy mobile homes mar rural landscapes in New Mexico, a sad testament to a lost skill of building with adobe, stone or logs.

Moreover, as they moved to a more modern world, in New Mexico, Colorado, California and Wyoming and beyond, they learned new skills, at first with some trepidation but with a fierce determination to succeed. As they acquired cars and trucks, they learned, first of all, to drive them, then maintain and repair them. As they confronted English, they learned, little by little, how to communicate in it, though they always preferred Spanish.

Cousin Josephine and her husband Sebastian Jacquez founded a successful real estate business while holding other jobs after leaving religious life as a nun and Brother, respectively. My brother Carmel established a landscaping business in Denver that provided a comfortable living for my father, Eusebio, for the rest of his life. Dad, then 55 years old, had been working for another landscaper, a Japanese American. But one day Carmel told him, let's go to Denver and start our own business. Carmel, a superb salesman with graduate study in education, would knock on doors, charm his way inside the house and soon come out with a contract. When the homeowner would say he or she needed tree pruning or building flowerbeds, Carmel would say, "Yes, we can do that," even as Dad would whisper to him in Spanish, "No, we just cut grass." Later Carmel would tell him. "We can learn," and they did.

Raymond Alle became a real estate broker even as he taught full-time at Illinois Central College. Now retired in Phoenix, he buys homes lost in foreclosure, repairs and re-sells them. There are few challenges that the people of Terromote will not tackle.

Celestino Aragon
(1931-)
(An oral history: 2005)

I was born in Creston, WY., but I was raised in Terromote, at Grandpa Octaviano's ranch. I went to the Perea school but mostly to the school in Rociada, where two little kids burned to death when a garage burned. We used to walk from here (about a mile and a half) to the highway where the bus picked us up. Clemente was one of the drivers. I remember that because when I came from the service I used to date his sister, Corine Sena.

In the summer, we used to take care of the sheep for Grandpa Taviano for a penny a day. We also took care of the cows and some-times lost them all; they went into the cornfields in *el valle*. One time that happened Leo and I had been playing trucks in the arroyo. When we got home, they told us: "You better eat supper because afterward we are going to kick the shit out of you." It was my brother Leo and I and sometimes Josephine. We all used to live here, in the house by the dam. I do not remember too much about that.

I lived in Terromote until I was 13, when I went to Brighton. I went by myself and I stayed with (uncle) George Olivas and (aunt) Dulcinea in a little house owned by Tio Eusebio. I stayed there three years, work-ing on the farm, in the celery and the strawberries. I used to drive a truck loaded with celery and strawberries to Denver to unload at the dock. I did not have a driver's license or nothing, but the guy I was working with was Japanese and they were pretty good farmers. I worked three years and, let me tell you, he did not pay me during those three years. He gave me only the money I needed. He saved all my money. So when I left and came here (to Las Vegas), I bought a new car.

On my 17th birthday, I went and enlisted in the service, (sent to Santa Fe for processing). A buddy from Raton and I flunked the IQ test. On them IQ tests, the more questions you answer, the more you have to have right. But the girl was really nice. She told us: "If you really want to go, I can fix it." So she made our IQ 80; you have to have 80 to get in. While in Santa Fe I went to the bathroom and met a guy (also enlisting) who had a little wine. We drank it and became friends. We were sent to Fort Ord, CA., and took basic training. Then we went to Japan for two years together. When the Korean War started, I had only two months left on my enlistment, but I got extended for a year and we were sent there. I spent 11 months in Korea. I got 11 months of combat pay

There were 3,000 of us on the ship coming home. When I got here, they called me to *The Optic* and I met another guy from here who had been on the same ship, Martin Maestas. After a three-week leave, I went to Camp Stoneman and Fort Sam Houston. So I served three years, but the extension meant I did not have to serve in the reserves. When I got out, I went back to Wyoming.

My family was living in Tipton, where my Dad was working. Dad was a worker. He liked to work and work. He died in Brighton, CO. My Mom and he are both buried there. I do not remember much about him because I was never home except when we worked in the section. But he worked in one section and I worked in another. So I worked in the section three years. During that time, I came to Las Vegas on a weekend, married Frances Lucero, and we went to live in Wyoming, but I could not make it there. We went to Denver where I worked for about six months for a company that made manholes, but I could not make it there either. So I left there and went to California, leaving my wife here in Las Vegas (temporarily). I worked in a furniture place for about six months and then I got a job in General Motors. I worked 23 years there. I started at GM in 1953 and got out in 1976 or 1977.

In GM everything is by seniority; at first you get the worst jobs. There were about 12 who got hired that day, and they were sort of prejudiced, which worked to my advantage. They picked up all the white guys for the assembly line, but they did not pick me. I was the only Mexican there. So I had it made. You see, the line pushes you. For about a year I repaired wiring harnesses. It gets boring because the days are so long. But at the same time I had a band. I played at the Three Kings in Hollywood, Gardenia, everywhere. One time I had 19 weddings lined up. We played songs from New Mexico and the people liked that kind of music. I played the saxophone and the guitar, then the keyboard. I just learned to play. I had a real good friend who taught me how to play the guitar. Then a guy who played the saxophone taught me. I learned little by little. I do not know why; I had the talent.

Then when I quit the band after 10 years, I had an upholstery shop. I learned upholstery when I went to Casper, WY., where my brother Lee had an upholstery shop and a filling station. He upholstered the truck seats for me and that is all I needed, to see him do it. I bought a machine and I learned it myself. I had six stitchers and ten sewing machines in my shop. At one time I used to make $1,000 a day doing government work. I used to get contracts from all over Los Angeles. I did all the upholstery for the main man at GM. I did not do it myself; I had two guys from Mexico who were really good. He told me he would put me on the line where they make the panels as the worker who would cover for absentees. "If everyone is there in the morning, you can go to your shop," he said. I had that for years. I really had it made. At the end I was doing nothing. I had a real nice job; I worked only when they went to eat.

I also used to do mechanic work when I was working for GM. I know everything about a car, though not these new ones. These new ones, forget it. You learn as you go along. It is like right now. I have a keyboard and each day I learn something new. It don't have no end, like the computer. I learned the computer by myself. I can fix the computer. I put a new hard drive in it, the motherboard, the whole deal (with a laugh). Anyway, in California I had this upholstery shop, for about 16 years. Then Sebastian, my brother-in-law, joined us and we bought a place; then I bought him out. Then we lived on a yacht for 10 years, but I made an upholstery shop in a van and I made canvases (for sails) while we lived in the marina after I sold my shop.

I sold my shop for $80,000. My attorney bought it and he fixed the paperwork to where he gave me so much and then he made the paperwork again and he put there that he gave me so much. He fixed the money part (to reduce the capital gains taxes on the sale.) When we were going to move here, the guy I sold the shop to, my attorney, I think he still owed me $12,000. He told his wife to make me enough checks, each for $500, to total the $12,000.

We also sold our boat for $10,000. My boat had two engines; it was a big job. Then not long ago they called me from California and the gal who owns the marina told me: "Joe, we have been asked to pick up your boat in Catalina." The guy who bought it had died from AIDS and he never changed the paperwork or nothing. When I sold it to him, he was single and he never changed anything. So the boat was still in my name. But I told the gal: "Go ahead and pick it up and I will give it to you." I did not want to go mess around with it. The guy who bought the boat still owed me about $5,000 and I lost it, but the boat that he gave me, a 23-foot Bayliner, was sold for $8,000 by the marina. We came here and bought 12 acres from my Uncle Herman at $2,000 an acre.

My marriage with Frances broke up a long time ago. I have been with this woman (Janice Sirbeck) for almost 20 years. But let me tell you something. Frances retired; she used to work for a company that made locks. This one (Janice) worked in a hospital as a bookkeeper. But I gave Frances the first chance. I told her: "I am going to retire and go to New Mexico; do you want to go with me?" You know what she told me? "I don't trust you." Then I went over to the hospital and told this one: "Do you want to go with me, but a sure thing; we are going to get together and stay together." She said: "Sure, just give me three months to quit my job. I will put you on my insurance at the hospital and we will fix your teeth." She was a nurse, a bookkeeper, everything, worked in a big hospital. She left with me and we got her mother, who is 91 and (now) in a home. We brought her here. [*The mother eventually died and, in 2009, Janice filed for divorce and returned to California.*]

I do very good in upholstery work here also, but I am quitting.

[*While he was in California, he upholstered a doctor's boat. As part of the deal, the doctor examined him and declared him partially disabled from the post traumatic stress disorder tracing back to his combat experiences in Korea, for which he began receiving $300 a month from the Veterans Administration*].

When I came over here someone told me to go see a guy in Albuquerque, a psychiatrist, a young guy. I took him some honey, and we had canned some vegetables and I took him a bunch. I went to see him and he fixed up all the paperwork (with the VA). He told them I was crazy. I am supposed to be crazy because you get crazy in the service. You have bad dreams. When we got to the hospital, first the nurse checked me out and did not find anything wrong, but the real good guy there said, Mr. Aragon, "I read all your paperwork here and as far as I am concerned, you are crazy, you're this, you are that and the other thing. The only thing I want you to do is help me is fix all this paperwork so we can make you 100% disabled." So I helped him fix up all the paperwork and then he said: "I want to go talk to Jan." He went over there and asked her, "Does he wake up at night hollering?" She said yes. He fixed all the papers to show that I was suffering from Post Traumatic Stress Disorder. I had gone to the Manchurian border and he needed to fix it so they could make it 100%. It took a year, but I got $32,000 back pay, my first check. They didn't find I was 100%, just 87% but every time you are over 70% they declare you 100%. I have been 100% for about eight or nine years (since he was 66 years old.)

So right now I get GM retirement, $318 a month after 23 years. Then I get $967 from Social Security and I get $1,000 a week for 100% disability. We have our home, our land and everything is paid up. Now we are enjoying it a little bit, but I like to work a little. I have arthritis and I have been raising honey bees. I was raising honey bees in my upholstery shop in California, but they shut me down because the bees are commercial, like livestock. I have been raising bees for about 30 years because I have arthritis and I read the encyclopedia about bees and it said the old timers used beestings for arthritis. So I tried it and when my knees start hurting I have a bee sting me. It hurts like hell for a little while but the arthritis goes away.

Celestino in retirement.

A lady comes from Albuquerque. The doctor told her he could do nothing for her arthritis but he told her about the bee sting. This gal's dad also had the partial disability (for military service) and it took him a long time to get 100% because he did not apply for it. So his daughter came here and I had a bee sting her, but just one to determine if she was allergic. I told her to come the next day if she was not allergic. She came the next day and I gave her five stings and she got well. But I told her: "Every year you have to get a booster." The bees are powerful.

This year I got 75 pounds of honey. Right now I visit all those people in Rociada. They all know me. I give them honey and they give me fruit. They have a lot of orchards over there. They give me plums and

I can them. Last year we made a garden. We had bundles and bundles of carrots. We canned 12 cases of 24 bottles. We have them under the bed. We do not eat that much. We canned maybe about 50 cases of vegetables.

In our family there is Josephine, then me, then Lee (Leo) (who died of diabetes), then Ben. When I moved to California Ben and Faby (Fabiola) followed me. Josephine, when she got out of the nuns, told me she was going to get married. I arranged the wedding for them in California, got her married and everything else. She and Sebastian have one daughter, (Yvette). Sebastian went into the apartment business, did pretty good. He just sold 23 units in California, got new trucks. They have a house in Rio Rancho (NM) and a bunch of apartments in Albuquerque. After Faby comes Mary Jane; she lives in Alaska. She married a guy from the Air Force, who was in Riverside but he moved to Anchorage, Alaska and retired over there. Teodorita lives in Cheyenne. Then comes Ernie, still in Colorado. I was born on Dec. 13, 1931. But I feel like I am 40. I feel pretty good.

I make as many appointments at the VA as I can. They fixed my teeth, made me a partial that I don't wear. I have an enlarged prostate and they gave me pills, urinating pills and Tylenol 500. They also give me arthritis pills and a baby aspirin. I go because they pay the hotel and give me $28 for gas. So we make as many appointments as I can in Albuquerque. On our way sometimes we stop at the casino. We do not go to casinos too much. We both sit at one machine. The only thing is that in the casino I smoke; I do not know why. We went to the casino about three weeks ago. I smoked a pack. I haven't smoked since then. Everybody seems to smoke at the casino. *(Continued in Chapter Eleven)*

Charlie Sandoval

(1959-)
(An oral history: 2004)

I was born in Rawlins, WY., and lived there until I was 11 years old, when my father was killed in a railroad accident. I am the fifth youngest of the 12 children; seven are older than me. The workers, all with big families, lived in houses that were very small and very poor, called section houses. We had no inside water. When we bathed we had to use a tub. I remember going to get water many times. It seemed like a long way when I was nine or ten, but when I visited as a grownup I

Charlie Sandoval in 2004.

saw that it was not far at all. My Dad bought me a wagon, and I enjoyed loading it with milk containers full of water and pulling it to the house. It was one of my happiest moments, but I generally have good memories of Wyoming: going through the *chamiso* with a good friend and playing in the haystacks, killing a skunk under our house with a stick, going out with my Dad, just the two of us, in a green station wagon so he could teach me how to drive. He would get angry when I killed the engine. I would see my Dad going to work every day. He never missed, never complained about his work, always worked very hard.

After my Dad died, we came to Las Vegas, NM. Coming from Tipton, a place with few people, it was a shock moving to a town 20 times bigger where we knew no one. It was hard and somewhat lonely leaving old friends behind and having to make new ones. My mother, the backbone of our family after my Dad died, faced the hard job of raising us and teaching us. We had to clean house, put food on the table; it was not easy. Sometimes we had no money. But when you grow up poor nothing really bothers you. What are people going to do to you? But if everything has been given to you, it's a big change.

I remember growing up eating tortillas, chile, beans, *papitas* (fried potatoes), peaches out of a can my mother opened. We always had clothes. My mother always had one room so immaculate that when people came it was always perfect. The entire house was clean, but that room was especially nice. Growing up in Las Vegas had its advantages. We are a close community, looking out for each other. There are few strangers; everyone knows everybody. Everyone gets along.

I graduated from high school and attended Highlands University for a couple of years but did not finish; college was not in my heart. I was already working and, having money in your pocket, you ask yourself: "What do I need college for? I started at Kentucky Fried Chicken when I was 17, and by 18 I was the manager, a job I held for eight years. Even when I was in college, I was managing the KFC. After that I managed up to 15 KFC's at one time, in Albuquerque, Farmington, Gallup and even places in Arizona. I learned a lot and that is why I am able to do what I do here. I went through a lot of technical schooling for six weeks at a time and then I learned by experience. I educated myself to operate my own business. I know how to be successful.

I stuck with KFC for 17-1/2 years, until I finally saved enough money to buy the Dairy Queen. I had saved a lot. I was there eight years and still own the Dairy Queen. For the past five years, I have been in this business (Charlie's Spic and Span Bakery and Restaurant), which has done very well. The lady who owned it before got into financial trouble and was going to lose it. She asked me if I wanted to buy it and I said no, thinking I could not afford it. I told her "no" two or three times, but she kept calling: "I want you to have this store; I am going to lose it." She said the banker told her I could borrow the money. I had a good reputation, known as a hard working person. It is not easy to be in business for yourself. You know, you have to sell yourself before you sell anything. I finally went to the bank and they gave me a good deal.

I took the restaurant to a different level, fine-tuning it, kind of turning it into a franchise. I brought the operational systems of KFC and Dairy Queen here. The bakery and restaurant were already here; tortillas were also made here, but they were rolled out by hand. I don't do that. This way (using a machine) you sell more tortillas, about 100 dozen a day. We make our own chile from scratch. I remodeled so we can serve 200 people up here (first floor) and 100 in the bottom. I have fed from 800 to 1,000 people in one day, in the restaurant and catering. We have a complete bakery in the back and built a new kitchen. I started the catering, for doctors, families, weddings, and other functions, groups of 25 to 500. We cook the food, deliver it, and serve it. We do it all.

Our motto is *Panza llena, corazon contento* (Stomach full, happy heart). People like it; tourists ask what it means. We have customers from many parts of the country. Some people come here every day. We are proud of what we do and try to make them feel at home. People love this place, our food and excellent service. How motivate the employees? Well, they are only as good as you are, working like the owner does. I love what I do and if you are happy at what you do, the employees are happy too. We have a good atmosphere, a good working environment, with good wages for our 33 employees here and the 15 at the Dairy Queen. We are like a family.

My wife, Elizabeth, has always been there for me. Of course, we have to raise the children, Isaac, 16, Carlos Ray, 14, and Elizabeth, 9 years old. My wife works in the bakery and in the Dairy Queen at lunchtime. I work every day but never miss my kids' activities. I have people come in to work at 4 a. m. and I get in by 7 a. m. and work 10 hours a day. When we cater a meal, I may have to work until 10 or 11 at night. It is getting to a point where we are busy all the time, though it is a little slow in the afternoon. That is when we do our remodeling, so we don't lose a dime. I have a manager to run the Dairy Queen. Sometimes I work two or three months without taking a day off. I am a workaholic. I am 45, the same age Dad was when he died.

We had two groups in the family, the older ones and the younger ones, to which I belong, along with Rita, a professional artist in Santa Fe, where she and her husband have a janitorial service; Julian and Raymond, who are in construction; Paul, an independent UPS contractor; Teresa, supervisor in a school cafeteria; and Rafael, who works here. But I have always been like the leader of the family. My mother always encourages me and is always there for me. My brothers and sisters have always come when I needed them. My grandmother, Carmelita Lucero, taught my mother how to make the best tortillas. We try to make them the same today. That is why I have a sign on the wall behind the tortilla machine saying: *"Tortillas como mi mamá hacía."* (Tortillas the way my mother made them).

I try to be a positive person, to think the good and not the worst about people. I look for the good, not the bad. I don't like negatives. We are probably the best restaurant in town, serving 500 customers daily. I am always looking for ways to improve it, installing new tile, carpet, tables, making sure everyone is happy, not just the owner. I tell my children: "Some day we are going to own a KFC, a Taco Bell and a Pizza Hut. We are going to own five restaurants." I want them to be active in them, but first I want them to get an education. That is a must. Of course, it may never happen, but, you know, it doesn't hurt to dream. I am always dreaming and often think of Martin Luther King, a man who dreamed of a better life for his people.

Ed Sandoval

(A work profile)
(Son of Octaviano "Tavianito" Sandoval Jr.)

When Ed Sandoval graduated from the Kansas City Art Institute in 1983, he wanted to be a fashion photographer. He therefore visited the major fashion markets in Chicago, Miami, Atlanta, St Louis,

Dallas, Phoenix, Las Vegas, and Los Angeles, where he photographed with the top modeling agencies. In Dallas he apprenticed for six months with a French fashion photographer.

Afterward, he opened a fashion/commercial studio in Kansas City because he wanted to be with his mother, Eleanor Garcia Sandoval, who was in the beginning stages of cancer. "I had a successful 2-1/2 year run there with another fashion photographer but knew that my talent lay elsewhere," he said. After his mother died in 1989, he spent another four years in Kansas City so he and his father could help each other deal with their grief.

In 1994, he and two other Kansas City photographers opened a studio in Santa Monica, CA. There he photographed many up and coming models and actors, including a then unknown Pamela Anderson, Tuc Watkins from the movie, "The Mummy Returns," comedian Tom Arnold and his greatest discovery, Sports Illustrated Model Chandra North. But because he found the Los Angeles lifestyle "a bit much," he moved to Phoenix in 1996, where he knew only one person.

There he opened a small home studio and met his future wife, Suzy Martin, at the time a hair and makeup artist. They built a 2500-square-foot naturally lit studio in the art district, complete with French doors and a dive in pool! In the ten years they were there, they had many commercial and fashion clients as well as local magazines, corporations and the Arizona Hispanic Chamber of Commerce. The magazines included Latino Perspective and Arizona Healthy Living; the corporations, Motorola, Holsum Bread Company, Starbucks Coffee, Village Inn, Dolce Salon & Spa, Courtesy Chevrolet, and America West.

Ed Sandoval and Suzy Martin in 2006.

"I got into food without knowing anything about it," Sandoval said. "A friend who had just opened a French restaurant asked me to do it as a favor. The photos came out so well that other restaurants were soon asking my friend Norman who the photographer was. So my business expanded from bikinis to biscuits and from runways to Subways. Now I often wonder what it would be like to photograph models in

Paris and Milan and the good restaurants there. So perhaps one of these days I will head for Europe and try my hand at fashion and culinary photography there."

For now, however, Sandoval and his wife, married for 13 years, reside in Springfield, IL., where he has a small model and talent agency. His main website, www.sandovalphotography.com, displays his work, as does www.illinoismodelsandtalent.com.

Photo Gallery

Eusebio and Amada Sandoval found happiness in hard work.

Raymond Sandoval, teacher, coach, and dean of students.

James Sandoval, an expert in finance, has worked in London and traveled to Kuala Lumpur and Israel in the course of his work. Based in Houston, he is the son of Moises and Penelope Ann Sandoval.

CHAPTER EIGHT

FIGHTING DISCRIMINATION

We met our first Anglo classmate when we began attending school in Rociada. He was a gangly blond kid, about 12, the son of a Texas cowhand who had just started working at the Pendaries ranch. The first day he came to school, he looked us over and said, "You are a bunch of dirty Mexicans." Cousin Johnny Romero walked up to him and asked: "What did you say?" The Texan repeated the epithet and Johnny flattened him with a single punch in the face. It was the last time our new classmate called us dirty Mexicans. Such triumphs did not prepare us for what we faced in Colorado.

The migration of New Mexicans to Colorado's South Platte Valley began with a few families arriving in the 1920s for seasonal work and returning home for the winter. Lee Montoya, from Cimarron, NM, started coming with his family in 1929 to work in the beet fields. When he married in 1938, he and his bride settled in Brighton, a small town with a sugar beet factory and a canning company in the midst of a rich irrigated farming area cultivating beets, peas, beans, cucumbers for pickling and onions. By that time, the New Mexicans were settling right away rather than going back and forth.

The first Pereas to settle in Brighton were Miterio and Hilaria Perea Padilla, from Manuelitas. Great aunt Casimira Aragon, her husband Dario and four children came in 1937. Uncle Filadelfio and Quirina Aragon, my mother's older sister, all from Terromote, came in 1942. Dad's cousin Manuel Padilla and his family, our family, that of Uncle George and Dulcinea Olivas followed. By the late 1940s, Terromote, Manuelitas, Sapello, Gascon, San Ignacio and Rociada, had representatives living in Brighton.

Brighton was settled in 1859 by homesteaders who saw the potential of diverting water from the South Platte River for irrigation. It became the seat of Adams County, near Denver. The settlers were Germans and Russians, many from Kansas, who needed the labor of Hispanics but did not welcome them as settlers. "The discrimination and segregation were so great that there were signs on the doors of barbershops, cafes and stores that read, 'White trade only,'" Montoya said.

Dr. James S. Taylor, in his monumental work on Mexican labor in the United States, quoted a beet grower in the South Platte Valley in Colorado who said in the late 1920s: "The Mexicans are an inferior race and we mustn't expect them to move up the scale in less than three or four generations." Hispanics suffered discrimination in all South Platte Valley towns, but Brighton was the only one with deed restrictions, which read: "These lots shall not be sold to people of the colored race or to people we know as Mexicans." Among the first to challenge and defeat those restrictions were the Pereas.

Once settled in Brighton, Montoya took a course in airplane mechanics in Kansas City but was never able to get a job. The school sent him as far as Detroit and Buffalo to interview for jobs, but every potential employer told him: "We do not hire people of Mexican descent." He finally became a mechanic and machinist during World War II but when he returned to Brighton from the Pacific he could find no job as a mechanic. Potential employers suggested he go back to work in the fields. So he started his own auto repair shop. Though his wife had to work in the fields during the first five years to save the business, the shop eventually became successful.

Little had changed by the time we arrived in Brighton. The Great Western Sugar Factory and Kuner-Empson Canning Co. hired only Anglos. My father would go to the employment office, fill out an application, and wait all day to be called; he never was. My brothers and I were always searching for part-time jobs, but no store would hire us. We had to set pins in the bowling alley and mow lawns. At St. Augustine Catholic parish we were welcome only at the 9 a. m. Mass each Sunday. In high school Hispanics were automatically placed in general studies and, in grade school and junior high school, there were assigned to the "C" group, the lowest of three tracks. At the Rex Theater, the only movie house in town, Hispanics were segregated in a "bargain section". Violence against Hispanics was common and, even in the 1950s, it was not always safe to walk the streets. Carmel, one of my brothers, was badly beaten by a carload of Anglos he had never seen.

Montoya, however, had won grudging acceptance and the city's leaders invited him in 1950 to run for the City Council and he was elected. But their hope was that he would help them to get rid of the growing Hispanic population. "Businessmen, one a banker, came to me trying to sell the idea that we should move the Spanish people a mile out of town and help them to build a community out there," Montoya said. "The businessmen said, 'Your people should be segregated by themselves. That way you could be together.'" Montoya refused.

As we settled in and gained confidence, we began to confront the discrimination. Soon, we were going to other Masses at St. Augustine, persisting in the face of insults and of sometimes being pushed out of seats rented to Anglos. The day came when we were welcome at all the Masses. When we had been in Brighton five years, I wrote a letter to Carl Doerr, editor of the twice-weekly Brighton Blade, protesting the segregation in the theater (see below). One day afterward, I was going by the theater and the manager came out and said he wanted to talk to me. He and his assistant took me into an office and demanded, "Whom are you fronting for? Who wrote the letter you put your name to?"

When I told them I had written it, they said: "You are a damn liar. A Mexican does not write like that." They shoved me around and ordered me to write another letter saying the first one was not true. They said that Carl Doerr had already agreed to print it and threatened to sue me if I did not write it. Frightened (and naive) I went to the state capitol

From left, Lucy, Ray, Cathy, Arsenio, Antonio, Elivinio; below, Carmel and Moises in 1969 after Eusebio Jr.'s funeral.

in Denver and asked to see the state attorney general. I waited about two hours but finally an assistant attorney general called me into his office. He told me gently that my problem was not one the attorney general dealt with. I had to see a private lawyer, which our family could not afford. But taking pity on me, he said: "Let me see the letter." When I showed him the clipping, he said: "Tell them to go to hell. They can't do anything to you."

I did nothing and shortly afterward, the manager of the Rex Theater was replaced. His successor told me Hispanics would no longer be segregated. "You and your family are welcome to come and sit anywhere," he said. It turned out that the Rex Theater was part of a chain, the Fox Theaters, and the main office did not know of the local manager's discriminatory policy until my letter was published. The old manager, by disbelieving that I was the author of the letter, made me aware that I could write well. Moreover, I learned that the printed word could be a powerful force for change. Those insights later led me into journalism.

When a plumber cheated my father, we refused to pay the bill. We were sued in what today would be small claims court. The judge at first refused to let me speak in defense of the family on the basis that I was not a lawyer, but I was finally allowed to present our side. We lost but legal proceedings did not intimidate us. When the gang that assaulted my brother Carmel was convicted, we sued for civil damages and won though we were never able to collect the judgment. In 1969 when brother Eusebio Jr. died from complications of unnecessary intestinal surgery our brother's wife, with our support, filed a lawsuit for wrongful death.[1] The first trial ended in a hung jury with all but one of the jurors in favor of the plaintiff;[2] the second trial was lost on a technicality. But we always felt the struggle was worth the effort. In the 1960s I was sued for libel for my investigative reporting exposing wrongdoing in City Hall in Albuquerque. I won the case. Then in the 1970s, cousin José Perea sued in federal district court against the discrimination he suffered at the Community College of Denver, where he was vice president. He won a $50,000 settlement.

More recently, Barbara Perea Casey, daughter of Uncle Lolo, sued when she was dismissed as superintendent of the West Las Vegas School District. She won a settlement of $250,000. Asked about it, she said: "My name is not just Perea; it is pelea (fight)."

A letter to the editor of the Brighton Blade
(Published July 25, 1949)

Mr. Carl Doerr
Editor of The Brighton Blade

Dear Sir:

"A fine place to live"–that is my opinion of the City of Brighton. But there is one spot that stands out like a sore thumb: the Rex Theater.

At the Rex Theater, the American doctrine, "Every man has equal rights," has been modified to "every man has equal rights–except all the people of Spanish or Mexican extraction. In order to do this, the management has divided the lower floor into two sections–the left-side section or "bargain section" where Spanish-Americans are required to sit and the center and right-side sections, where all other Americans sit. The "lower-floor" section price of admission is 60 cents and the "bargain section" admission price is 50 cents.

As I am a Spanish-American and in order to beat this segregation policy, I have been buying the higher-priced ticket and sitting where I see fit; but the management has now prepared for that too. Recently my brothers and I went to the Rex Theater with the intention of enjoying a good show. Three of us bought tickets for the "lower-floor" section, entitling us to sit anywhere on the lower floor. The usherettes, however, demanded that we sit on the left side of the "lower-floor section." After much discussion we were permitted to sit where we desired. My other two brothers, accompanied by a small German-American friend, bought children's tickets and sat on the "lower-floor" section. The usherette immediately moved my two little brothers to the "bargain section," leaving their German-American friend in the lower-floor section. Not willing to submit to this un-American treatment, we requested our money and left.

Is this the American way? Discriminating between the blond American and the brunette American? Refusing equal rights to people because of difference in nationality?

Yes, I know that there are a number of people of Spanish extraction who do not deserve to be granted admission into the theater. But that does not make all the Spanish-Americans bad. That does not warrant the discrimination which prevails in such a fine American community.

As loyal and true Americans, it is the duty of the people of Brighton to make the Rex Theater an example of the American way. The Brighton Blade can do much to make Brighton's theater a better place of entertainment for all the people of Brighton, regardless of race, color or religion.

I shall appreciate your reply.

Sincerely yours,
Moises Sandoval

Dr. José Perea

(An oral history continued from Chapter Six)

In 1972, I became Dean of General Studies at the Auraria campus of Denver Community College. When I got there my desk was in the hallway of a building that used to be a car dealership. Someone took my jacket, which I had put on a chair, and put it on a dog and took a picture that appeared in the school paper with the caption: "The new dean is a dog." The faculty could not see a Chicano as dean. Some of them were very abusive. But I eventually took hold of the situation, got my office and established the position of dean of general studies.

A year later, in December 1973, I became vice president of the Community College of Denver and chief executive of its Auraria campus. I was selected through a "screening committee" that reviewed applicants and then an interview committee that interviewed seven applicants. The committee ranked me as number one and recommended me to the president, Leland B. Luchsinger, noting my strengths as awareness of minority concerns, contact with the Auraria Higher Education Council, instructional strengths, personality strengths, poise in tough situations and vocational program awareness. The only weakness was depth of experience in front-line administration.

But from day one of my three-year tenure, I was hounded by the then president of the college. He demoted me to a non-existent position, vice president of minority programs. A desk and a telephone were provided in the sitting room of a storage area next to the toilets. Although I continued to receive my salary as vice president, I had no secretary, no budget and no authority. My complaint of discrimination, filed in 1976, finally came to trial before Judge Richard P. Matsch in Federal District Court in Denver in 1979, and I won a complete victory. He ruled that I was "forced into the role reserved for minority groups through all of human history–that of a scapegoat." He concluded that I had been the victim of "invidious discrimination" (See excerpt from his decision.)

Nevertheless, because of the turmoil the conflict has caused, with faculty and administrators taking sides, I felt I could not reclaim my position of vice president even though by then Luchsinger had left to accept a position at Colorado State University. I accepted a letter of apology and a settlement of $50,000 and returned immediately to my beloved New Mexico.

[In Las Vegas, Perea got a job as vice president of Luna Vocational and Technical Institute, the first year only a research project paying $17,000. Then he served as vice president of administration for six years and then as superintendent of the Las Vegas city schools for another four years. In retirement, he taught an occasional course at his alma mater, Highlands University.] (Continued in Chapter Eleven)

Excerpt from Judge Richard Matsch's decision in the Perea case

"From the evidence presented, it seems apparent that President Luchsinger never really accepted Dr. Perea as being adequately qualified for the responsibilities of Auraria Campus Vice-President. It also is fair to say that his acceptance of the interview committee's recommendation of Dr. Perea for that position was more of an attempt to accommodate the demands of Chicano students than it was an administrative choice. It could perhaps best be characterized as a reluctant recognition of the realities of time, place and circumstance. That reluctance developed into a consistent pattern of increasing emphasis on accountability while decreasing authority and acceptance. The manifestations were many. On each occasion when Dr. Perea recommended the appointment of persons to become deans or division directors or for other positions of responsibility, President Luchsinger questioned their qualifications and asserted that he would hold Dr. Perea personally responsible for the acts of such appointees, most of whom were minority persons....

There is a significant contrast between the perception of the Denver Community College Auraria Campus administration made by the evaluation team for the North Central Association of Colleges and Schools in November 1974 and that made by President Luchsinger in 1976. The evaluation team said:

The campus administration is made up of individuals who are apparently dedicated and industrious. Throughout the administrative structure there is a discernible attitude of concern, thoughtfulness and candor in approaching administrative responsibilities. The present chief executive officer of the Auraria Campus utilizes an extremely open style of leadership based upon accessibility to other administrators, faculty, staff, and students. Input is encouraged from all levels in all segments of the College community. (Plaintiff's exhibit 14, page 15)

That evaluation team also foresaw the difficulties which did later arise at the Auraria Higher Education Center (AHEC), urging that the central administration recognize that the time involved in coordination with the other institutions at AHEC imposed a particular burden on the administration of the Auraria Campus and suggesting that a different approach might be used in the relationship of that campus to central administration from that of the other campuses.

That was not done. The central administration showed a gross insensitivity to the particular needs of the Auraria Campus. Dr. Perea's administration was compared unfavorably with the North and Red Rocks Campuses without any apparent recognition of the conditions and circumstances which were sufficient to separate them.

In his criticisms of the Auraria Campus Vice-President, President Luchsinger repeatedly and continuously placed such emphasis on accountability for all actions of subordinates that he seemed to be following a militaristic model. His approach was such that it could be said that the philosophy of Clausewitz had replaced that of Dewey in education. But with all of that accountability there was no correlative authority. Dr. Perea was not free to speak for his school at Auraria Executive Committee (AEC) meetings. The president often intervened directly in the affairs of the Auraria Campus. He was not at all supportive of his vice-president there.

When the financial-aid to students crisis developed, José Perea was forced into the role reserved for minority groups through all of human history—that of a scapegoat. The finger of fault was pointed toward him, not to the Dean of Student Services whose responsibility it was and not to anyone at the central administration.

In attempting to justify the removal of Dr. Perea as vice-president, President Luchsinger said that he had lost faith in the plaintiff as an administrator and he sought to support that conclusion with examples including the financial aid problem. Considering all of the evidence as a whole, those reasons must be considered to be pretextual. What is most persuasive is that President Luchsinger and the State Board artfully avoided any opportunity for Dr. Perea to confront the factual issues through a grievance procedure by using the mechanism of a reassignment. If Dr. Perea could not handle his administrative responsibilities, what justification was there for placing him in another position with the same pay and stature? That action was taken while an EEOC complaint was pending and that would appear to have been another reason to avoid any opportunity to present a defense to Luchsinger's charges. In fact, it could be inferred that there was an element of retaliation in that move. Such a substantial departure from normal administrative procedure is very strongly suggestive of an intent to treat Dr. Perea differently and, in the absence of any other explanation for such an abrupt maneuver, the fair inference is that this man was the victim of an invidious discrimination.

This case is the functional equivalent of a discriminatory termination of employment. Cf., Young v. Southwestern Savings and Loan Ass'n., 509 F.2d 140 (5th Cir. 1975). While a reduction-in-force because of financial exigency would clearly be justification for discharge, here the reassignment set up the termination. The position of campus vice-president was not expendable. The position of vice-president for minority affairs, created as a shelf upon which to place Dr. Perea, was a convenient place to cut and it was also convenient that a reduction-in-force termination could not be the subject of a grievance procedure. Again, confrontation on the facts was avoided."

---

[1]During an exploratory procedure, the surgeon took out the gall bladder prophylactily and performed other procedures that expert witnesses (surgeons with the same specialty) declared unnecessary.

[2]The dissenting juror agreed with the others but would not vote against the surgeon because she thought he had done a lot of good during his life.

CHAPTER NINE

TRIUMPHS AND TRAGEDIES

When Uncle José Dolores (Lolo) Perea woke up one night in 1967 with severe intestinal bleeding, he was rushed to the hospital in Las Vegas, where an exploratory operation revealed that there was nothing that could be done to save him. So he called in Aunt Julia, his wife, and gave her instructions on what to do. Then, as his life ebbed away, he worked on the crossword puzzle from the daily newspaper as he did in his normal routine. That is how he spent his last moments.

Danny Suazo, a great grandson of Enrique Perea, (see below) died trying to shield an employee from the crazed husband who came to kill her at the large grocery he managed. Patrick Perea, a locomotive engineer, (see below) witnessed a bank robbery in 2007, chased the bank robber, captured him with the help of two other men and sat on him until the police arrived. In the Sandoval and Perea families, there are many inspiring sagas like these.

But there are also moments of failure that all of us wish we could live over. In my own family, the children of Amada Sandoval, me included, lacked the wisdom and compassion to fulfill her last wish: that she not die in the nursing home where she had been sent after her last hospital stay for a failing heart. We did not realize until later that it's not death that terrifies; it's dying at a place not of one's own choosing.

A lesser failure but one that stirs sadness in retrospect occurred in 2005. On a Sunday afternoon in April, we had a party for my Uncle Herman Sandoval's 92nd birthday, complete with dinner, music and dancing at Cousin Charlie's Spic and Span restaurant in Las Vegas. My brother Arsenio and I paid half the cost, the other half paid by Uncle Herman's daughters. None of his five sons came. People said it was because alcohol was not being served, although there were also other issues. One son-in-law, Arturo Vigil, was there. Many of us had had difficulties with Uncle Herman over the years. One time he drew a pistol and forced me and José Perea

Herman Sandoval dancing with granddaughter at his 92nd birthday party in 2005.

to stop surveying a parcel of land that belonged to Perea. But I helped pay for the party and went to New Mexico to be there because it was time to forget the past. As it turned out, that birthday party was the last opportunity for everyone to reconcile.

Serving alcohol was out of the question because many of those present had had a bad experience with alcohol. Twenty-five years back, Arsenio had reached the point where he said the choice was continue drinking and die, or quit and live. He chose the latter. By then he had lost everything–job, tenure as a college professor, house and, later, his wife. There were people at that party who had had experiences they did not want to revisit, in actuality or even in memory. The husband of one of the daughters had died in domestic violence involving a gun and alcohol or drugs. Cousin Irene Sandoval had been married to a man who beat her when he got drunk. At least two of Uncle Herman's sons had had problems with alcohol. One of them, Jimmy, died two years later at the age of 49. Many lives, both in the Sandoval and Perea families had been diminished by alcohol.

Alcohol had cut short the life of my brother Carmel, the fifth oldest brother in our family, who died when he was 50 years old. It was a great loss because he was bright, optimistic, and always full of good ideas. He always told us not to undersell ourselves, which we often tended to do. He had been a college professor, an official of the National Education Association and a businessman. A labor contracting business he founded provided a good living for his widow after he died. But he loved to drink and could not give it up.

Irene Sandoval's second son had been killed in a one-car crash on Martin Luther King Drive in San Francisco after partying all night for his younger brother's birthday and then setting out, at 4 a. m., to buy cigarettes. José Perea's father Pedro gradually drank himself to death at age 66. But other lives were affected by alcohol. Maria Katie Sandoval, Irene's sister, never married because she could not trust the men she dated not to drink, smoke or use drugs.

Catching a Bank Robber

[The hero is a great grandson of Enrique Perea.]

Little did Patrick Perea, locomotive engineer, know that Feb. 9 (2007) would end with him sitting on a criminal who was accused of robbing seven banks in the Albuquerque region.

Perea and his daughter, Jessica, were standing in line at a Wells Fargo Bank in Albuquerque when a man in front of them handed the bank teller a note, reached over, grabbed approximately $3,000 in cash, shoved it into a bag and left.

He (Perea) heard the teller yell that she had been robbed, so he took off after him (the robber).

"This is my neighborhood. I will not let the criminal element move in," Perea said.

Perea and three others caught the suspect in a nearby parking lot and Perea sat on him until police arrived.

The suspect stood accused of seven other bank robberies in Albuquerque and Santa Ana, CA. According to court records more than $8,000 had been stolen.

"There was a feeling of elation for the simple fact that we did catch him and seeing that there

Patrick Perea

were more people around who helped out," Perea said. "They felt the same way I did and cared enough to get involved."

Perea, 48, has been with the railroad for 30 years. "I enjoy the responsibility of the work we do on the railroad," Perea said.

Jessica was proud and excited for her father and what he did.

"It was an adrenaline rush for all of us," Perea said.

From Southwest Express, publication of the Southwest Division, BNSF Railway.

Arsenio Sandoval

(An oral history)
(Continued from Chapter Six)

In Oak Creek, CO, I had two experiences that influenced my future. I met an alcoholic priest who taught me about sophisticated drinks. Then one day I slapped a girl who pushed me and, as a result, the school board decided not to renew my contract at the end of the year. I quit right away and joined the Army, in 1957.

Sent to Korea, I worked in Seoul at the army's education center. I met my future wife, Chun Hi, there. One day I saw Chun Hi walking on the base and followed her home. She invited me into her house. We started going out and then living together off the base. It was love. I extended for three months and married her before coming home in 1959.

In Brighton we lived with the folks for about three months, until I got a job teaching at Meeker Junior High School in Greeley. Then in 1960 I accepted a grant to study at the University of New Mexico for a master's in Spanish with applied linguistics. Our first daughter, Ruthie, was born on Aug. 14. The following summer during a conference in Washington, D.C., I met nuns from the College of St. Teresa in Winona, MN. They offered me a position teaching Spanish and I taught there for seven years. The rest of our children were born there: Steve on July 7, 1962; Patty on Nov. 14, 1963; and Maria, on July 31, 1965. While there I joined Toastmaster's International and won the speech contest one year. But then my wife's schizophrenia became a big problem; she had to be hospitalized often, once for six weeks. She had started to hear voices when we lived with my folks but was fine in New Mexico, where I finished the work for my master's during the summer of 1965.

A few years later, with my wife's condition worsening, I moved back to Colorado. My brother Eusebio Jr. had won a fellowship to study for his doctorate at the University of Colorado but died in 1969. I took the fellowship instead and finished all the course work for a doctorate before my alcoholism became a problem. Then I taught seven years at my alma mater, now the University of Northern Colorado, won tenure and bought a home. Then things fell apart.

Because of my drinking, the dean handed me a letter of termination, saying I had to move on at the end of the year. I immediately went for treatment at a place claiming it had a cure. They let you drink all you wanted after giving you a shot so the alcohol would not get into the bloodstream. You got bloated and threw up. When I returned the termination was rescinded. But after I got thoroughly drunk to celebrate, I got the letter again. I was on unemployment for a while before the college found me a job teaching at Johnstown High School. But because I continued drinking and missing too many classes, I lost that job and my home as well. Once again, we moved in with the folks.

One day after we had been there about six months, my mother said to me: "Son, we are tired of you; we want you to get an apartment." I replied, "I don't even have the money to put up the down payment." She said: "I will lend it to you. Go away." I rented a house on 3rd Avenue and started going to a program (AA) to help me stay sober. I would sober up for months at a time but I would always end up drinking again.

On August 21, 1981, my mother's birthday, as I remembered later, I had drunk myself into a corner and I recognized that I had only one choice left. Either I would keep drinking and die, or stop drinking and live. I chose to live. But I knew I had to finish that drunk. I went to the Jam Bar in Brighton and I drank for five straight days. When I walked out on August 25, I was finished. I have been sober ever since–26 years.

My wife and I were still together for about two more years. We lived in an apartment on 18th Street. Our marriage, however, did not survive my alcoholism and Chun Hi's schizophrenia. We got a divorce. She now gets care for her illness in a group home and I take care of mine by faithful attendance at AA meetings.

Then I started going with a nurse named Becky Young, a divorced mother of two children from different husbands who was 36 at the time I met her. I married her, but she was addicted to prescription drugs and died from an overdose when she was 38.

Meanwhile, sober now, I had gone back to teaching in 1981, this time at Brighton High School. I did not have much of a retirement fund because every time I lost a job I withdrew my retirement funds. But I got a chance to buy back my retirement and since I was earning $40,000 a year, I bought back 10 years at a cost of $17,000, paid it in two years. I thought to myself, "As soon as I have 20 years I am out of here." I did not enjoy teaching high school students. Their main priority was developing social skills. I retired from Brighton Public Schools in 1992, but continued working at Aims College to increase my retirement pay. Once I retired, there was nothing to keep me in Colorado. For four years I came here (New Mexico) by myself, as my current wife, Jan Hurst, was reluctant to move. But I finally convinced her. I went into debt when I came here because I put everything on credit cards. I still haven't paid off the credit cards, but I'm making headway.

I keep busy here in New Mexico. I am an adjunct professor at Luna Community College in Las Vegas. In 2000 I was chosen "Teacher of the Year in the State of New Mexico in Continuing Education." I now teach Spanish for Health Professionals in the Nursing Department.

I have become a songwriter, copyrighting 28 songs. I have made several CDs. My songs play on several radio stations, including KOCA in Laramie, WY. I have also performed live at KOCA and KNMX in Las

Vegas. And I play with Los Cuatro Amigos, a band of old-timers specializing in the old music of New Mexico.

I do a lot of fishing with my cousin, José Perea. I guess you can say I'm happy as a lark living on the ranch. One of my songs, *"Nuevo Mexico Querido"* says it best,

> *"Your purple mountain majesties are all beyond compare,*
> *Your montes are enchanted, there's magic in the air,*
> *There is more beauty here than anyone can speak,*
> *And if you don't believe it, just look at Hermit's Peak."*

Maria Katie Sandoval
(1949-)
(An oral history: 2005)
[Daughter of Alfonso and Dora Sandoval]

I was born in my grandfather Octaviano's ranch in Terromote on July 7, 1949. For that reason Matthew 7:7 has been my favorite passage from Scripture. If you want to know who I am, read Matthew 7:7. [The passage goes: "Ask and you will receive. Seek, and you will find. Knock, and it will be opened to you."] I got my desire to learn and go to school from the same teacher in Las Vegas who inspired my older sister Irene: Gabina Griego, my first grade teacher. I would also see my aunt's sons, Adam and Chris, studying and typing and I liked that. But like my other brothers and sisters, I had to go to many schools because our family kept moving back and forth between Las Vegas and Wyoming.

After I finished the first grade my father decided to move to Wyoming. We went by train, my parents and us six children. I had a little pink dress, handed down to me from my aunt's daughter. They could not sit me with the others because we were too many. So they forgot me on the train when they got off in Rawlins. Since it was like 1 a. m., I was sleeping. The conductor awoke me: "Little girl, little girl, are you going to Rawlins?" I said no because I remembered my father saying we would be living in Tipton. The conductor took me off the train at Rock Springs; otherwise, I guess I would have gone all the way to California. Meanwhile, my parents missed me as they were settling in a little house. My father ran to the foreman's house and he called on one of those old fashioned telephones. My Tia Juanita had to drive my dad to Rock Springs to pick me up at the station, where I sat asking: "Where are my

Mom and Dad?" They wrote about me in the newspaper in Rock Springs. After that my family called me "la perdida," the lost one.

In Tipton where I went to a one-room school, I was the only second grader and there were only two third graders. For the third and fourth grades I was back in Las Vegas. We moved back and forth several times, but for the eighth grade I attended junior high in Rawlins, WY. Then it was back to New Mexico for the 9th grade where I attended West Las Vegas High School, applied for cheerleader even though I was very shy and was elected captain. I stayed with my aunt for the 10th grade because my parents had once again moved to Wyoming, but because I missed them a lot I went to Wyoming for the 11th grade. But I dropped out because there was a lot of prejudice at Rawlins High School and went to live with my sister Irene in San Francisco, where I attended an adult school. But I got scared when my brother-in-law, though nice to me, was mean to Irene when he drank and I decided to go back to New Mexico. In Las Vegas, I found I had enough credits to graduate with my class.

Katie Sandoval at the ruins of the house where she was born.

I was the first one in my family to graduate from high school. But I did not think I could go to college or that my parents could afford it. So, not liking Wyoming even though I missed my parents terribly, I went to Albuquerque where I got a little stipend through the Peace Corps to go to a technical and vocational school to become a bilingual secretary. After that, being too young to go to South America with the Peace Corps, I went to work for the Albuquerque Public Schools.

At school I met the young man who would become my daughter's father. He got a job as an apprentice in electronics at Sandia Labs and we went together for three years, but I did not think he would make a good husband. He wanted to get married right away, but I didn't. I remembered how upset my mother had been when my sister Irene had become pregnant at 15. When I became pregnant at 23, we broke up, though we remained friends for three more years. It was difficult, two losses at the same time, because that's when my dad was killed.

When I heard Dad was killed, I went to Las Vegas so I could travel to Wyoming with my uncle Herman and aunt Simona. We went by Greyhound. I was like a zombie and a woman sitting nearby asked me why I was so sad. I told her and she gave me a little book, like a novella, which I still have somewhere. I prayed and prayed and I guess it helped me. My dad was proud of me because I never did anything that would get him upset. He used to say I was his pet. He was a beautiful singer and every holiday he was there with his guitar. He could also play the banjo, saxophone and the violin. He danced polkas; all of a sudden he would be jumping around.

When my daughter was three years old, I moved back to Las Vegas and enrolled at Highlands University. My mother helped me, babysitting my daughter while I was in class. I eventually got my Bachelor of Science degree in mental health, did my practice with an agency that cared for the mentally ill, and then went on for a master's degree. Now I am a mental health practitioner for Lovelace in Albuquerque.

When my daughter was in the third grade, I learned she was a gifted child; she was placed in a special program until the 6th grade. She was married at the age of 23, has two children and a degree from the University of New Mexico, earned by attending evening classes.

Looking back, I did not want to get married because many of my brothers and sisters got married very young. It's not that I wouldn't want a partner; of course, I would, and I have gone out with men. But I can't deal with smoke or drink; I am like my father. He never smoked or drank, even coffee. The only time he brought liquor was for the holidays, a bottle of Mogen David wine, and he would share it with all of us. It was our little tradition. I rarely drink liquor.

Excerpt from a May 17, 1996, column in the National Catholic Reporter by Moises Sandoval

I grew up on a farm where we had rifles, used to hunt or to kill farm animals for the family table. But taking human life is another matter. I remember the feeling that came over me when I was first issued a rifle in the Army and I realized that I might have to use it to kill human beings. Yet countless thousands of Americans who carry concealed weapons seemingly have already crossed that Rubicon.

Loaded guns pose a danger not just to real or imagined enemies one might face in the streets but to their owners' families as well. A report by the Children's Defense Fund, cited in a Christian Science Monitor editorial, reveals that in 1983 2,951 U.S. children died from gunfire. In 1993, 5,751 people under the age of 20 died of gunfire, a 94 percent increase. More preschoolers were killed by guns in 1993 than police officers or U.S. soldiers shot in the line of duty. Most of the deaths occurred in the home.

A recent issue of Woman's Day carried a full-page ad from a group by the name of Cease Fire. It had a picture of a pistol with a tag that said: Suburban Dallas, TX, 15-year-old female killed by 10-year-old brother with gun found in parents' room. Boy thought gun was unloaded, tried to scare sister as she talked on phone.

Reports such as these gain my attention because two of my cousins died from gunfire in the past year. On April 28, 1995, Danny Suazo, 37, was killed at the large supermarket he managed in the Denver suburb of Littleton. Auto mechanic Albert Petrosky, 36, armed with a big-bore bolt action .50-caliber rifle, a second rifle with a detachable 30-round magazine and a 9mm pistol similar to those issued to the police, burst into the store in pursuit of his estranged wife, Terry, 37, the deli manager. He had already wounded the woman who drove Terry to work. As Suazo tried to help her get behind the service counter, Petrosky shot him three times. He killed his wife and then Sheriff Sgt. Timothy Mossbrucker, 36, who was shot before he could get out of his police car. Mossbrucker's wife was expecting the couple's sixth child and Suazo had four children, all under 14. Petrosky, convicted of first-degree murder of the officer and second-degree murder of Suazo and Terry Petrosky, told police he went crazy for a while. *[He committed suicide while incarcerated.]*

On Oct. 6, 1995, another cousin, Michael Angelo Perea, 31, of Colorado Springs, CO, and his wife, Martha Elena, 26, came home from work on a Friday night in a festive mood. Both worked for the Colorado Corrections Department at the state prison in Canon City. They went to dinner with friends, each had only one drink and left for home about 11 p.m. They seemed happy and at peace. But a short while later they were dead.

Deliberately or accidentally—no one will ever know—Perea, who worked as a security officer at the prison, shot and killed his wife. Then he telephoned a brother and, finding he was away on a business trip, told his sister-in-law what he had done and indicated he was taking his own life. The sister-in-law called 911, but when the police got there, it was too late.

The House of Representatives recently voted to repeal the assault weapons ban passed earlier in the Clinton administration. At least 13 states have passed concealed weapons laws. But as arms proliferate, life gets more precarious for everyone.

The Day My Grandfather Died

By Rita Vega-Acevedo

[Vega Acevedo is a great granddaughter of Octaviano Sandoval and the wife of a physician in South Pasadena, CA].

My Grandfather Apolinario Padilla was six feet tall and so hand-some that heads turned wherever he went. He was a trader and bartered goods when he was not tending his small ranch in Terromote. My grandmother Carolina often went with him to neighboring villages.

During World War II, he and his family drove to Oakland, CA in a scene reminiscent of the "Grapes of Wrath." Traveling with their belongings piled on the back of a truck, they joined relatives who told them about plentiful jobs. Both grandparents worked in the shipyards to help the war effort. The Padilla girls attended school and learned how to get around in the burgeoning city. "It was one of the happiest times of my life," my mother, Conferina, remembered. "I even learned how to take the trolley to school."

In Oakland, my grandfather saw a world he had never imagined. He explored the city, went to western movies, bought men's suits and starting wearing a fedora hat. He brushed shoulders with people of different races. "Before leaving New Mexico, my father didn't think women should go to college," my mother said. "When he returned to New Mexico, he told skeptical friends that his daughters should get degrees. He had changed in California."

But Grandmother Carolina became homesick and convinced the family to return to New Mexico. They settled in Las Vegas but often went to their small ranch in Terromote. "No one imagined that my father would be dead three years later," my mother said.

On September 27, 1948, Grandfather Apolinario was driving home from the ranch with a friend. As he went to pass him a $20 bill, it flew out the open window. He stopped the truck alongside the gravel road and got down to look for it. Father Walter E. Cassidy, the pastor at Our Lady of Guadalupe in Sapello, was coming along the same road in a truck pulling a load of metal plates on an open trailer bed. As the truck passed by my grandfather, the trailer hitch broke and the metal plates flew off the trailer and slammed into my grandfather's chest.

A local rancher and other men placed my grandfather's bleeding body on the flat bed of his truck and sped 12 miles to St. Anthony Hospital in Las Vegas. As they went down the two lane highway full of dips and valleys, the men attending him prayed silently.

My grandfather was pronounced dead on arrival at 12:30 p.m. and the cause of death was declared to be an accident, but my family was not satisfied. "Afterward, we did not hear from the Catholic Church," my mother remembered. "Neither the church nor Father Cassidy sent us a letter of apology. My mother was not compensated in any way." On

Apolinario Padilla and his daughter Conferina in 1946.

that fateful day, my mother was a 17-year-old senior in high school. She was pulled out of class to go to her mother's side. "I knew something was terribly wrong but I didn't know what," she said.

After the accident, according to my mother, Cassidy drove himself to St. Anthony Hospital in Las Vegas and was admitted, presumably to deal with the trauma of the accident. "Later, I heard that he wanted us to visit him at the hospital," my mother, a 79-year-old retired teacher said. "He wanted forgiveness. We could not forgive him. My father's death robbed his daughters and grandchildren of his presence in their lives."

[The family felt it did not have the full truth of what happened. Now, sixty years later, Vega-Acevedo is trying to find the answers.]

CHAPTER TEN

RELIGION'S INFLUENCE

In a sense, Enrique Perea was as responsible for our going to college as he was, by building a school on his own farm, for our learning to read. Had religion not been so important in his life, his daughter Amada might not have desired so strongly that her son Antonio become a priest and therefore should go to college rather than to an electronics trade school. Once Antonio started college, the rest of us followed.

Among Enrique Perea's children, his younger daughter Amada was the one most like him in terms of religion. When we moved to Brighton, all but one of her sons, with her strong encouragement, became altar boys. We took the Confraternity of Christian Doctrine classes offered in the parish. Although the Sisters in the parish thought I had a vocation, Mom told me I had to help the family, which I was happy to do because I did not in fact have a vocation. Antonio, the second brother, was the one she wanted to be a priest. But he did not have a vocation. Two other brothers, Carmel

Eusebio and Amada and their seven sons in their altar boy cassocks and surplices.

and Jay, did enroll in the junior seminary of the Theotine Fathers, but that strict Spanish order soon sent them home, for disciplinary, not academic reasons: too rowdy.

Religion was also responsible for what we became, for three of us graduated from Catholic colleges or universities and two others attended for a time. Only one, Elivinio, had the benefit of a Catholic high school education, a scholarship student at Cathedral High School in Denver. He went on to Regis College and then to Creighton University, where he received his degree in dentistry.

In my case, I went to a Catholic university not only to get what I had missed in not going to Catholic schools (there were none where we lived) but also to find a wife of my own faith. The education I received at Marquette influenced my choice of journalism, and to work for a

Catholic publisher in Ohio and the Catholic Foreign Mission Society for 30 years. At Marquette I met the woman who became my wife, Penelope Ann Gartman.

Religion eventually led Antonio to become a permanent deacon in full-time ministry. But religion giveth and religion taketh away. He gave up a brilliant career in chemistry for a deacon's poverty, having to devise novel ways to earn a living at it. Nevertheless, as a person of faith would say, the Lord provided. His three children graduated from college, the youngest from Harvard, and the oldest went to law school and became a lawyer. But it was not easy, because wife Maud, a PhD in microbiology, also gave up teaching to work in ministry with her husband.

Cousin Josephine Jacquez embraced a life of poverty as a Franciscan nun but for her the impetus to choose the religious life came from Aunt Ignacita Sandoval (see below). From an economic standpoint, life had a different outcome than for Antonio. After being dispensed from her vows after 20 years as a nun, she married a former Jesuit Brother from Mexico and they became prosperous in real estate.

Religion, but not Catholicism, changed the lives of others. Richard and Anna Perea, children of José and Stella Perea, became members of the Unification Church. They were married in a mass wedding in New York, their spouses chosen by the founder of the church, the Rev. Sun Young Moon. For Richard, Moon chose a Japanese wife, Masako; for Anna, a German husband, Fritz Schneider. For a time, Richard was the publisher of the church's newspaper in New York City, then manager of the church's flower business in Miami, Florida. Anna and her husband Fritz were missionaries in Botswana and Guatemala.

The Schneiders now live in Rio Rancho, NM, where she works at Intel as a manufacturing technician and he works in sales and management for a company in Santa Fe. Richard and his family live in Miami, where he is president of Landmark Investment Co. and travels widely in Latin America. Masako works at home. Neither Richard nor Anna worked for a church organization in 2009.

The children of Josie Aragon and Joe Montoya became evangelicals.

Dr. Elivinio Sandoval

(1935-)

[Son of Amada and Eusebio Sandoval]

I was the top student in the eighth grade in the Brighton Public Schools, had straight A's in every course. When I got my report card, I showed it to one of the Victory Noll Sisters who worked in our parish. We knew them well because seven of us were altar boys. She looked at it said: "Gee, you merit a scholarship to a Catholic high school in Denver. The Archdiocese pays full tuition for the best eighth grader in every parish." I knew nothing about the Catholic high schools, had not even thought about them. Call it luck, fate or God helping me, I was at the right place at the right time.

The Sister arranged everything and I chose Cathedral High because it was the easiest to get to. I had a 44 mile commute each day, 22 each way. I got a ride from someone going to work in Denver. Sometimes I was dropped off a long way from the school and had to walk a mile or two and take a bus to get there. Sometimes I missed my ride home and, having no money for the Greyhound bus, had to ask a Sister or one of my lay teachers to lend me enough for the fare. Sometimes I had to wait a long time for my ride home, but that worked to my advantage. I did my homework while I waited. It seems hard now, but we had more spirit then. We felt there was always a way.

I finished at Cathedral second in my class by a few hundredths of a point. The top student, Bob Carver, got a scholarship that paid half of the tuition to Regis College, in Denver. But he chose to go to Marquette and I got the Regis scholarship. A Protestant missionary organization paid the other half of my tuition. Since my grades were high enough, the scholarships were renewed each year.

When I graduated, I was accepted by all three of the dental schools to which I applied: Creighton, Marquette and St. Louis. I chose Creighton because it was closer and the cost of going back and forth was less. When I graduated I owed only $1500. I was frugal. Nowadays, the typical dental school graduate owes more like $150,000.

Throughout my life I have had the sense that I was at the right place at the right time. Even my promotions in the military came at the right time, especially the one to bird colonel. I had very good rapport with the officer who was going to write my report. He advised me to become involved at the base and in the community. I did as he suggested and was promoted.

It seems that things go right if you try to be a good person and have the right attitude and ambition. But besides being qualified you have to be likeable enough that people will want to do things for you.

I think all of us were aided by the great independence and initiative we gained in New Mexico. We were optimistic, liked to work and always tried to be the best, not easily accepting second place. We sought to adhere to Christian principles: prayer, church, charity and love of neighbor. Our parents taught us not to steal, to be good kids, stay close to the church and to help others. I make the mortgage payments for my son Patrick, daughter Christina and brother Frank. I do it because I can and because they need a little help.

Antonio A. Sandoval

(An oral history: 2006)
(Continued from Chapter Six)

When I was ordained a deacon, on June 11, 1973, I became more interested in church work than in teaching chemistry. In October of the same year we went to Belize to do mission work. When I asked for a year off from the University of Missouri in Kansas City, we had been invited to go to Brazil to do Marriage Encounter. And of course when a deacon goes to do church work he must have the bishop's permission. We were going to a center that had a lot of industry and I thought I might work there as well as do the marriage encounter. However, the bishop took so long that my time was going by and I was still in Kansas City in September, with no job and no income. But I met a deacon from Central America–Paul McCardle was his name–and he said, "Why don't you come to Belize? We need a teacher down there." He gave me a telephone number and we called there, talked to the principal of the school, Sister Clarita Vasquez. I asked her, "When do you want us to come?" And she said, "Right away."

So within a week we were on a plane, the entire family (wife Maud, children Carlos, Eusebio and Amada), including a Pomeranian dog and my mother-in-law. I started teaching right away and did marriage encounter on the weekends, and functioned as a deacon also. Paul McCardle and I were the only two deacons in the whole country. It was a very exciting time. Within nine months we had started the marriage

From the Children's Educational Fund newsletter, Dec. 21, 1994:

In June we were nominated for the El Pomar Excellence Awards for our work in the non-profit sector. We sent in the information requested and subsequently were informed that the Children' Educational Fund, Inc. was not one of the finalists. Later we were invited to the Awards Luncheon in Colorado Springs.

That day several non-profit organizations received awards for their work in a variety of areas. Near the end of the program, they changed master of ceremonies. The new one then said, "Every year we give an award to an individual for leadership in the non-profit sector; this year we are going to give it to a couple, Drs. Antonio and Maud Sandoval." We were shocked, but grateful. They gave us a trophy and $15,000.

We were asked to give $10,000 to a charity of our choice and to keep the other $5,000 for our personal use. We gave the entire $15,000 plus an additional $5,000 to the School District for a scholarship fund from which the interest will be used each year for a scholarship. We had to put our treasure where our heart is, with the students we are trying to help.

While it is great to receive recognition of the excellence of our work, we have frequently remembered the words of Rudyard Kipling, "If you can meet failure and success and treat these two impostors just the same, then you are a man." We needed to share this good news with you, but we also want to put it behind us so that it will not detract us from the "Giver of the Gift" and the work we still have to do.

encounter movement in Belize and from there the people we trained took it to Guatemala and to the Caribbean. I was there one year.

I came back to the University in 1974 and taught there until August of 1980. Then I gave up tenure, retirement—everything—to do ministry full-time.

[In an article in Revista Maryknoll, Maud wrote this about their decision: "My husband and I, typical in many ways, wanted financial, professional and civic success. Also since before our marriage, we participated together in the Legion of Mary and social action projects. But as the years went by, tension developed between our desire for success and our yearning for a deeper involvement in serving oppressed peoples. Ultimately, we concluded that we could not 'serve two masters.'"]

During a visit to the Mexican American Cultural Center in San Antonio, I met Father Prudencio Rodriguez, a Vincentian priest, who said, "Come to Denver," and gave me Auxiliary Bishop George Evans's name. We called the bishop and he was very helpful. Since we had no job and no income, he got a lawyer who donated his services to help us set up the St. Jude Missionary Society, a non-profit through which we raised the funds to carry on the work. At first it was mostly with migrants, then as the coordinators of the parishes with prayer groups. Then in 1983 when Renew started we were made the coordinators for all the 17 parishes in the archdiocese with Renew in Spanish. Eventually, we began teaching English as a second language (ESL).

In 1987, we began experiencing difficulty in getting assignments from the director of the deacons, Father Mark O'Meara. Realizing we had to do something else, we met with an attorney who said, "I have a non-profit organization that we could use." That was the Children's Educational Fund (CEF), originally started in 1969 to help low income minority students in Catholic School, later adding Headstart. A nun by the name of Rosemary Keegan ran the program. But one day in 1987 she was assaulted and left incapacitated, in a wheel chair for the rest of her life. We reactivated the CEF to do ESL classes.

Maud and Antonio Sandoval in recent photo.

In 1989 when O'Meara refused to give me assignments, we went with the Children's Educational Fund. Without an assignment in the church we couldn't raise funds through any organization for church work because we were not in church work anymore. That made the St. Jude Missionary Society defunct.

[Antonio never learned why O'Meara refused him assignments and incardination. But on the day the priest died in 1999, another called him and said: "The king has died. If you will apply, you will get your diaconate license."][2]

We got a contract with Weld County School District 31 to coordinate a family education program consisting of ESL classes for adults, and pre-school classes, tutoring for students from fifth grade through high school. We did this with the assistance of the University of Colorado, which provided the tutors. Initially, Headstart provided the pre-school classes and later on ESL, with a grant from the same school district, that we kept going until 1998. In the beginning I got a job with the school district as a case manager, with a grant from the Colorado State Department of Education, and this was with students who were really having academic problems. At the same time we were invited to participate in seeking a grant for drug abuse prevention. The grant was funded, administered by the University of Northern Colorado. For five years, between 1990 and 1995, we worked on that grant in four school districts. Then we were on our own.

At that point we began to do the ESL classes. We had a building (donated by the G.I. Forum in Ft. Lupton, CO), and my brother Arsenio taught the ESL classes. In 1998, we began to do the classes ourselves. During our stay at Weld County we started a Mathematics, Engineering, and Science Achievement program (MESA) seeking to prepare women and minorities to enter college in science. Gloria Nelson and John Rael ran this from the University of Colorado at Denver. We had a tremendous record. The kids were given special experiences, taken on field trips to Hewlett Packard, Martin Marietta, Boeing, colleges and universities. Inspired to go to college, about 95% of them did go, not all of them in science, but a very high percentage of them were Hispanic and African American. Young women went into science. MESA began in California; a retired military person named Garcia, working for an oil company, started it in Colorado. He did a great job. Though open to anyone wanting to participate, the directors and staff were asked to recruit Hispanics and other minorities specifically. We contacted persons with good grades with the potential for a college education.

Our struggle at the time was to get teachers to recruit students. At that time we were still working on the drug abuse prevention program and we had many programs, in sports, acting in plays, and one in Tae Kwon Do. One day, noticing a young girl, I asked her if she was in high school. She was and her grades were excellent. I talked to her about MESA. One of the directors of MESA had her in a geology class. She sat in the front row and had excellent grades, but he never invited her. I invited her and she joined. Her name is Sofia Diaz and she went on to do well.

After 1998 I taught ESL until 2004. After I finally received a diaconate assignment at St. Augustine in Brighton in 2000, I still kept the ESL classes because I had no income from the church. Though I asked the pastor, income did not materialize. At the end of 2002, Alfonso

Sandoval, who succeeded Father O'Meara as the director of the deacons' program, called me to see if I would accept the post of assistant director of the formation program. I asked him if it carried a salary and he said no. "We assume that you are retired and don't need it," he said. I told him I did need a salary. So I turned that down. A few weeks later, he called to tell me there is a parish in Commerce City that lost a deacon abruptly (gave two weeks' notice and left) and the job did pay a salary. Even then we kept the ESL classes, until December 2005, when we stopped altogether. Eusebio, our son, taught for three years, but what derailed it for us was that the school district started giving free classes. We were charging what amounted to $1 an hour. Right now I am thinking of selling the building and concentrating our activities in the parish where I am a deacon.

Josephine Jacquez
(1930-)
(A profile based on an interview in 2003)

Josephine, the oldest of Conrado and Juanita Aragon's nine children, was born on May 2, 1930, at Grandfather Octaviano's farm. Her parents were then living in Wamsutter, WY, where Uncle Conrado worked

Ignacita and Josephine.

as a track laborer, but Juanita wanted her first child to be born at home. Afterward, she took her first-born back to Wyoming where the family lived for the next 11 years. The Aragons returned to Terromote after Pearl Harbor, when several of Juanita's brothers went to war, leaving Grandfather Octaviano short-handed on the farm.

While living at her grandparent's home, Josephine received the religious formation that led her to become a Franciscan nun, the only woman from Terromote to enter religious life. The first stirrings of a vocation came when she met Victory Noll Sisters who came to Rociada to prepare the children for their first Holy Communion. At home she was impressed by the practices and traditions of her grandparents. "At Christmas we would rock a cradle with a statue of the baby Jesus for hours and the grownups would give us candy and apples," she recalled.

"On Sundays, we went to Mass on a little truck owned by Uncle Tavianito. It had a railing on the box in the back and we rode there. They always gave us two nickels, one to put in the collection basket and one to spend. We stopped at a little store where we could buy a bag of peanuts for five cents. In May and October the grownups made little altars and our job as little girls was to get flowers for them. Then everyone prayed the rosary, which always seemed to take a long time. When it did not rain, my Grandmother, Grandfather, Dad, Mom, uncles and aunts took a small statue of San Ysidro and walked around the fields in a little procession."

Josephine, her younger brother Celestino and her husband Sebastian in 2005.

Like other young women in Terromote, she often went to help the neighbors. "I used to help my Tia Amada when she was going to have a baby," Josephine said. "We put a blanket on the table and my cousin Moises ironed on one side and I on the other. He did the sheets and pillowcases, anything that was easy, and I did the shirts and pants. I never expected any payment. I was happy to hear, *"¡Qué mujercita eres!* (What a little woman you are) or *¡Qué buena trabajadora eres!"* (What a good worker you are.)

"One time when Tia Amada went to the hospital to have a baby, I came by and asked Uncle Eusebio. *¿Quiere que le haga tortillas?* (Do you want me to make tortillas?)

"*Sí,*" he replied.

"How much flour should I use?

"One cup."

"One cup made only four tortillas, which the family ate in no time. So the next day I came by again and asked Uncle Eusebio if he wanted me to make tortillas and how many cups of flour I should use. He replied: "As many as you want."

Josephine no doubt was inspired by her mother, who loved to go help others. But there was a down side to her social activity. Josephine had to babysit her brothers and sisters, wash floors on her hands and knees, cook, make bread and iron clothes. What she disliked the most was to wash diapers, which had to be done using a tub and washboard. Josephine could not envision living the rest of her life that way.

However, the key influence in her becoming a nun was that of Aunt Ignacita, the housekeeper for the parish priest in Sapello. He often left her alone to go to distant chapels where he said Mass and stayed overnight. She wanted someone to come to live with her. "I asked if I could go and my parents said yes," Josephine said.

Tia Ignacita always prayed that someone in the family would become a Sister or a priest. She enrolled Josephine at Immaculate Conception School in Las Vegas. A school bus picked her up every day. "I admired the Sisters and felt I wanted to be a teacher like them. When I graduated from the eighth grade, the pastor, Father (Walter) Cassidy, arranged for me to enter St. Francis Convent in Santa Fe."

Josephine's parents took her there in June of 1946. The Sisters, a Franciscan congregation from Switzerland with a motherhouse in Colombia, South America, told them not to return to visit for six months, the length of the postulancy. She felt inferior "because we had been poor and spoke another language. But later I said, 'I am going to be what I am and if people do not accept me that is too bad.'"

She found convent life rather difficult. In her high school classes she got into trouble if her grades were too good–made her proud rather than humble. But she finished high school in three years with very good grades. She thought she would be sent to college; instead she was sent to another convent to help in the kitchen and work in the laundry, the fate sometimes suffered by other Hispanic women who entered religious life. She was content because she thought it was God's will.

A year later, with four other Sisters, she was sent to Immaculate Heart College in Texas. After a year there and two semesters at Our Lady of the Lake College in San Antonio, she was sent to the Panama Canal Zone to teach second grade. She was there for 10 years, not allowed to visit her parents even once. She earned a college degree by taking correspondence courses during the summers while in Panama.

Her next assignment was in Hereford, TX, where she taught the fifth grade and substituted for the principal while she was away in college. Then, following a retreat, she was assigned to work in Amarillo, TX.

"Then Vatican II came and they said all you had to do was love God and your neighbor. Some of the Sisters stopped going to meditation.

Then some took their habits off. The community divided between the older ones who did not like the changes and those who did. Four years after Vatican II, many began leaving the convent." Josephine, then 37 and a nun for 20 years, disliked the new ways more and more. She asked for a dispensation from Rome, got it six months later and left in 1967. She received $500 for living expenses. "I had given God the best years of my life. I decided I could still live a good life close to the Church and teach."

While in Amarillo she had met a Jesuit Brother, Sebastian Jacquez, who left his order six months before she did. Both settled in California, where they married and had one child. "I was already 39 when I had Yvette," Josephine said. The daughter, educated in Catholic schools, owns a successful marketing business.

A welder, Sebastian became the manager of a ten-apartment complex where he worked until he retired. A year after their marriage they had saved enough to buy an apartment with four units. Then they bought a house they remodeled themselves. Before long, they bought two other houses plus a home in Downey where they still live. They added many other units later, in the Los Angeles area and in Albuquerque.

Josephine taught in Catholic and public schools until her retirement in 1995. Then she worked part-time at an ecumenical center where she counseled women who were contemplating abortions. She was the only bilingual counselor and the only Catholic. Some of the women decided to keep their babies after talking with Josephine. "I enjoy working with such God-loving people," she said. "I have seen many small miracles. Helping there gives meaning to my life."

---

[1]Maud Sandoval, "Serving one master," in Revista Maryknoll, May, 1981, p. 8.
[2]Moises Sandoval, *A History of the Hispanic Church in the United States* (Maryknoll, N.Y., Orbis Books) 2006, p. 113.

CHAPTER ELEVEN

MILITARY SERVICE

Since the beginning of the 20th century, men from Terromote have served in every war involving the United States. During World War I Uncle Isabel Sandoval fought in the trenches in France and died from the effects of poison gas after he came home. Uncle Filadelfio Aragon also served in France but returned home in good health.

Uncles Ben, Octaviano Jr. and Herman Sandoval served in World War II in India, the Pacific and Europe, respectively. George Olivas and Geraldo Martinez, husbands of two Sandoval aunts, Dulcinea and Elis, , also served in the military during World War II, as did Joe Montoya, the future husband of Josie "Fefa"Aragon.

Octaviano Sandoval Jr. served during World War II.

Montoya, born in San Ignacio, volunteered during World War II and served with the 5307th Provisional Unit, later known as Merrill's Marauders. This all-volunteer unit was assigned to defend the Burma Trail deep behind enemy lines. One of only several sharpshooters in his platoon, Montoya was selected to be the personal bodyguard for a Colonel Beech and other high-ranking officers. After contracting malaria and being wounded in battle, he spent a few weeks recuperating in a U.S. hospital. While returning to rejoin his platoon, the ship was destroyed by an enemy torpedo. Montoya and other survivors spent three days in the water before being rescued. Of the 5,000 members in the 5307th, fewer than 1,000 survived the war, Montoya among them. He followed Josie, his childhood sweetheart, to Brighton, where they married, raised two daughters and four sons. He worked for the federal government for 37 years, dying in 1988.

Cousin David Alle, a professional military man, fought in Korea, as did cousins Celestino Aragon, José Perea and his brother Jacobo. They were in some of the fiercest battles. Celestino and another soldier were the only survivors of the 30 men in their platoon. In José Perea's unit, only seven of 48 men came back.

Dario Aragon served during World War I.

Sergeant First Class David Alle, a paratrooper, won the Silver Star in Korea, the Bronze Star and Gallantry Cross with Bronze Star in Vietnam, the Purple Heart for wounds suffered in Unsan, Korea on Nov. 30, 1950 (See below). His last assignments were with the 82nd Airborne and Special Forces. He was serving in Thailand when he died, on Jan. 25, 1974, from a massive heart attack.

Cousin Alfonso Sandoval Jr. also served in Vietnam. My brother, Antonio Sandoval, already with a doctorate in chemistry, was an Army private who never had to wear a uniform. He served in a special unit assessing the radiation damage done by the nuclear tests at Eniwetok Atoll in the Marshall Islands.

Another brother, Dr. Elivinio Sandoval served 20 years in the Air Force's Dental Corps, attaining the rank of full colonel before he retired. Another brother, Arsenio, served in Korea after hostilities had ceased. I served during peacetime in the Army's Corps of Engineers as a lieutenant and, in the reserves, in an armored unit, for a time as company commander of a headquarters and service unit. José Perea's son Jimmy, who was also in the Corps of Engineers, fought in Iraq during the first Gulf War and cousin Gilbert Perea, son of Uncle Lolo, served in Saudi Arabia during the same time.

Many others with roots in Terromote also served. As far as the author knows, all served honorably and all came home, but José Perea's older brother, Jacobo, returned psychologically damaged and could not resume a normal life. After years at a Veterans Administration hospital in Colorado, he died at the age of 32. His death was declared a suicide, but José suspected that he was murdered.

Dr. José Perea

(An oral history continued from Chapter Eight)

After basic training in 1950, I was sent to San Antonio for eight weeks of study to be an operating-room surgical technician. Then I was sent to Japan, where a hospital was being opened. But within two weeks the Inchon landing took place and plans for the hospital were cancelled. I was sent to Korea, assigned to the 15th Infantry Medical Service of the Third Infantry Division of the Eighth Army but attached to a machine gun company of black soldiers in the Third Battalion. Only the officers and the medical people were white. I knew no one.

On Nov. 7 we made an amphibious landing at night at Wonsan, North Korea, in weather below zero and were placed in the perimeter of the Fifth Battalion of the Third Division eight miles from the Chosin River. That's when 1-1/2 million Chinese attacked. As soon as that happened, our division was ordered to march to the rear and set up a defense perimeter around Hungnam, a port city on the eastern coast of North Korea. We were hit every night but held the perimeter until all United Nations troops and 100,000 civilians passed through our lines and were evacuated by ship from North Korea. After that was accomplished, on Dec. 23, our Division was ordered to destroy our weapons and ammunition, abandon the perimeter and march to the shore.

On Dec. 24, under enemy fire, we boarded landing craft in what was called a "reverse amphibian action." When we got to the ship we had to climb up rope nets. At the top, two huge sailors picked me up and threw me about 10 feet onto the deck. I streaked into the shower before they could put guards to stop anyone else from going in. Then we ate our first full meal since landing in Korea, standing at narrow tables where we placed our trays. The best part was a big bowl of ice cream. Then I found a corner on the deck and went to sleep. I did not wake up until the ship docked in Pusan. We remained there two days resupplying and then they marched us north into battle again against the Chinese, who had crossed the 38th parallel and advanced into South Korea.

The machine guns were never in reserve. Whole rifle companies went on reserve but not the machine guns. We had 48 men in the machine gun platoon and when I left only eight of the original group remained. Normally, soldiers went on R&R after two months on the front lines. I had to stay on the fire line for six months. The officers at the aid station, located behind the lines, simply forgot about me. They saw me only when I came in for supplies. Nobody knew me. Finally, we got a new lieutenant for the machine gun platoon, and he asked me: "Have you gone on R&R?"

"No, I have been here since we landed," I replied. He called up the aid station and chewed them out. He told me to pack up to go on R&R for five days in Japan. About an hour later, he came back and told me to pack up all my baggage. "You have enough points to go home. You are going back to the States."

I returned to the U. S. in June of 1951 and finished my three-year enlistment at White Sands Proving Grounds. I got out in March of 1953.

SFC David J. Alle
(From the National Personnel Records Center, Military Personnel Records)

Special Awards received by Sergeant First Class David J. Alle during his service in the U.S. Army:

Silver Star for gallantry in action against the enemy on 12 October 1950 near Hanpo-ri, Korea. While SFC Alle's platoon was engaged in crossing a bridge to establish positions on the other side, it was mistaken for the enemy and forced to seek cover by a strafing attack of several friendly planes. Realizing that many casualties might be inflicted on his platoon if the attacks were to continue. Sergeant Alle voluntarily and fearlessly disregarded his own personal safety to remain in the center of the bridge and wave his helmet in an effort to attract the attention of the attacking pilots. Despite the machine gun bullets striking his immediate vicinity he refused to leave his self-appointed position until he had drawn the pilots attention and the strafing ceased. Sergeant Alle's quick thinking, extreme courage and selfless action in the face of intense fire was responsible for saving the lives of many of his comrades. His gallant actions reflect great credit upon himself and the military service.

The Bronze Star Medal for distinguishing himself by meritorious service in connection with military operations against a hostile force while serving as Airborne Training and Parachute Maintenance Advisor, Airborne Division, Army of the Republic of Vietnam. His performance of duty was in keeping with the highest traditions of the United States Army and reflects great credit upon himself and the military service.

Gallantry Cross with Bronze Star presented by the Government of Vietnam. SFC David J. Alle disregarded danger before the enemy anti-aircraft and zealously provided supplies and re-supplies for battle, assisting the units in winning over the enemy.

Purple Heart for wounds received in action in Unsan, Korea on 30 Nov. 1950.

Celestino Aragon

(An oral history continued from Chapter Seven)

We were the first ones in Korea. We were in a delaying action. The enemy came across the 38th parallel. Then we went across twice and they drove us back. I was 11 miles from the Manchurian border. That is how far we went up there when the Chinese came in. We hit them with everything we had. I was pinned down one time for eight hours by machine gun fire. In my outfit, of about 3,068, there were only 86 of us left, but my friend and I were lucky. He saved my life when he got shot through the leg above the knee. The lieutenant told me to take him to the CP and there an officer told me to wait until morning before returning to my unit. That night my platoon was completely wiped out, all 28 men in it. We were in the Chosin peninsula until they brought in replacements. After that I was one of the first ones in rotation.

Photo Gallery

Author, then in Reserve Officer Training Corps, and his future wife, Penny A. Gartman, in 1954.

Colonel Elivinio Sandoval, Air Force Dental Corps.

Isabel Sandoval's tombstone in the cemetery by the chapel of San Isidro. He served in the 89th Division in the First World War.

Herman Sandoval served in Belgium during World War II. The Army, in its wisdom, made him a barber and that was fine with him. He was already married and a father when he was drafted.

CHAPTER TWELVE

BRIGHTON'S DEEP IMPRINT

In New Mexico we never went to a barbershop, principally because the family could not afford to but also because the closest barber was 20 miles away in Las Vegas. Our parents cut our hair. When we moved to the South Platte Valley town of Brighton, however, my father had less time and energy to do it. Also, as teenagers, we desired a professional cut and could earn enough doing part-time work to pay for it. But there were no Hispanic barbers in town and the Anglo ones cut our hair in poor humor. I will never forget the day I was sitting in one barbershop waiting my turn with two other Hispanics. Suddenly, the door opened and a large man in work clothes poked his head in and asked: "Hey, Jesse, do you have a full-house?" The barber gave him a lopsided grin and replied: "No, but I have three of a kind."

I moved away from Brighton more than 60 years ago, returning only to visit family, but the memory of that exchange remains engraved in memory, as does my first day at Brighton High School in 1944. We had just moved there that spring after I graduated from the eighth grade at the four-room school in Rociada, NM. Brighton High School was many times larger. Because I did not know my way around, I was late to my first class, general science, taught by William Gamble. As I walked in, everyone laughed, even the teacher. I have never forgotten the sound of that laugh, the kind that greets the sight of something totally unexpected, perhaps like the entrance of a dog. Few Hispanics went to Brighton High School at that time and those who did soon dropped out. Miss Olive Carr, the civics teacher, regularly warned against eating tortillas, something I still remember when I eat them.

I also remember the day my brother Carmel was walking down Fourth Street when a car screeched to a stop and a gang of Anglos he had never seen punched and kicked him. Similarly, I can still picture Frank Bucci, the grower we worked for during our first summer in Brighton, saying, "The Mexican is incapable of anything beyond common labor."

Discrimination left an indelible imprint and its effects took a long time to overcome. The sharp slap of rejection could come when you least expected it; you had to be on guard all the time. When we were with Anglos we were very quiet; it was our protective coloration.

Seeking acceptance, we did not speak Spanish other than at home. I remember pleading with Mom while we were at the grocery store, "Please do not speak Spanish. They are giving us dirty looks." But she was not intimidated. "I don't care; Spanish is my language and I am going to speak it everywhere." She insisted everyone should accept us the way we were.

Although discrimination can crush, it can also goad you to try harder, to refuse to be discouraged. Rudy Baca, whose family worked alongside ours many times in the fields, said that every time he was discriminated he would silently promise his tormenter. "Some day I will be as good as or better than you." By the 1970s, he was assistant principal of North Junior High School in Brighton.

Overcoming our timidity, we learned to speak up and to ask questions. That impressed an accountant who one time visited my high school bookkeeping class and he spoke to me afterward, planting the seed that led me to college. We also learned to be persistent. When I began college at Colorado State University in Fort Collins, paying my own way, I needed two jobs. So I went door-to-door in the business section asking for part-time work. I was turned down dozens of times, but I finally found a machine shop that hired me as a part-time bookkeeper and a restaurant that gave me a job washing pots and pans in exchange for my meals.

The most important lesson we learned was that, though many people in Brighton were biased, there were also good people disposed to do the right thing. A young Anglo who knew us took down the license number of the car belonging to one of the gang that assaulted my brother Carmel. He called police, who apprehended the assailants. At Brighton Junior High, the most coveted honor was the American Legion award given to the outstanding eighth grade graduate. My brother Elivinio, who eventually became a dentist, set his sights on it and worked very hard to win that distinction. The Legion Post gave him the award, even though some of its members surely wished an Anglo had won. At Brighton High School, I was among the 13 students chosen by the faculty from a class of 85 for induction into the National Honor Society and my peers elected me the group's vice president. Respect had replaced the derisive laughter that had greeted my arrival four years before.

In the 1960s when I returned to visit my family, I was amazed at the progress made by our people. Cousin Benny Padilla, a neighbor in

Terromote who had come to Colorado with his family to work in the beet fields, now lived in a modest white frame house with blue trim on South Fourth Street in Brighton. The house was paid off and he had an $800 color TV in his living room, a new pickup and a late model compact car in his driveway and a camping trailer on the well-cared lawn of the back yard. He had become a concrete finisher, earning many times what he received as a farm worker. He wanted his six children to have the chance he never had—to get a good education.

Another cousin, Arthur Aragon, had joined the Air Force after his high school graduation, worked as a milkman when he returned to civilian life and now was a bookkeeper for Navajo Freight Co. in Stockton, CA. His sister, Teddy (Mrs. William) Suazo, who was in my high school graduating class, was a homemaker with five children and worked as a secretary for the Adams County Welfare Department. Her husband worked for National Biscuit Co. in Denver and they were buying a new home in the suburb of Northglenn. Their oldest son, Harold, had recently graduated from high school with honors and won a four-year scholarship to Regis College.

Then in 1977 when I received an Alicia Patterson Foundation fellowship to study Hispanics, one of my projects was to find out what happened to the families that had worked alongside us in the fields in the late 1940s, I found that those people of northern New Mexico whom I call the people of the whirlwind had put their own stamp on Brighton. Though the Anglo in Brighton had not yet fully accepted the Hispano, the city now had four Mexican restaurants and a tortilla factory where a few years before there were none.

At the Police Department, Sgt. Art Quintana headed the community relations unit. He began working in the fields at the age of four but walked off at the age of 16 to do odd jobs in town, cleaning bars and restaurants. As other children of the poor, he had missed too many days of school but, after his discharge from the Army, did attend college for three years, worked as a recreation counselor and then joined the Police Department. When he was offered a more lucrative job by a bank, the city manager and police chief persuaded him to stay. But Quintana said the Department still received calls asking: "Please send an officer to my home but don't send a Mexican. I just don't like Mexicans."

One day the previous fall, Policeman Rudy Vialpando had been sent to investigate a complaint that a resident was burning trash in violation of city ordinances. The officer, according to his sergeant, told the Anglo offender that he had to give him a citation. He replied:

"You write me a citation! A Mexican write me a citation! You know, if it were not for me, your parents probably wouldn't have survived because it was persons like me who put your mother and father to work."

At the high school, the principal was a former dropout, John Nuanes, who had been a year ahead of me. He quit in 1947, a few months before he was scheduled to graduate, so as to join the Army, where he served 20 years, including a stint as a sergeant in intelligence. He went to college at night and by the time he retired he had his degree. He carried mail for a while and then taught school, meanwhile continuing his studies until he had a master's in secondary school administration. Then he became assistant principal and finally returned to Brighton as the top administrator in the same high school where as a student he had been refused admission to the Spanish Club because he was Hispanic. For him too, the discrimination remained etched in memory. He recalled being ostracized by fellow students because he had to wear bib overalls. "To this day," he said, "I do not own a pair of jeans."

Lee Montoya, the New Mexican who had struggled so hard to start an auto repair shop, now said he had to turn business away and 75 percent of his customers were Anglo. Invited by the city's leaders to run for office in the 1950s, he had served 11 terms on the City Council, ten years of which he had the title of assistant mayor. He had gone door to door seeking signatures on petitions for city services in the neglected northeast barrio where Hispanics were once forced to live. Then he had fought hard to get them approved by the Council. It was his proudest accomplishment. The city had named Lee Montoya Park in his honor and he still served on several city boards.

Nevertheless, electing Hispanics to the City Council had not become easier. The previous fall, Brighton had held a City Council election that, in one district, pitted an Anglo against an Hispanic, Max Rodriguez. Terry Lucero, an honors graduate of Brighton High School and now the director of a recreation center, stood outside the polling place all day and counted Anglo and Hispanic voters. At the end of the day, his tally showed 20 more Anglos. Immediately, before the votes were counted, he informed Rodriguez, "You lost by 20 votes." The count revealed Rodriguez lost by 17! Only one of seven city councilmen was Hispanic.

Though by then going to the barbershop was not the frightening experience it was when we moved to Brighton, the most successful barbershop was the Matador, on South Fourth Street, owned by Phil and June Trujillo, originally from Gascon, NM, in the same area as Terromote. They had started out in a tiny rented shop on Main Street and had had great difficulty getting zoning approval to build their own shop on Fourth Street because it was to be part of their home. Because the barbers association shunned them, they dropped out and set their own prices, higher than the other shops. But they got more customers anyway, perhaps because the Hispanics, now more than a third of the population, felt more at home.

Slowly–too slowly–relations improved between the Anglos and Hispanics, but there is a sense in all of us that an unreckoned price has been paid for it. Educator Ray Romero (see profile below) said back in 1977: "I feel that the young Anglo is much more receptive to us as Chicanos, probably because we are much more Anglo than we were 30 years ago. I hope we don't become completely like them, but we are learning many of their ways, traditions and values."

Lucy Sandoval Branch

(1944-)
(An autobiography by the first daughter of Amada and Eusebio Sandoval, born in Brighton, CO, three months after the family moved from New Mexico.)

Spanish-Americans is what they used to call us back in the late 1940's and 50's when I was growing up in Brighton. Even in the very early 60's we were still Spanish-Americans. On my birth certificate, my parents' race was noted as "White." Suddenly, sometime in mid 60's and 70's there was a Chicano Movement going on and we had suddenly become Mexican-Americans. We were no longer classified as members of the White race. We were led to believe that aside from the three major races since the beginning of mankind on this planet, there now was a

Lucy growing up in Brighton.

new race. Anyone of Spanish decent was now a member of the Hispanic Race.

When my pregnant mother and her seven sons boarded a train in Las Vegas, NM, in 1944, and headed for Brighton, CO, I was not yet born but I was with them on that little meandering train chugging its way to the place that would transform the entire family from descendants of Spaniards who settled in northern New Mexico in 1693 to a family of educated college graduates. Many doors opened up for our family, including for my father who worked a myriad of jobs before learning to drive at age 43 and starting a landscaping business when he was 55. Finally, he had a job that made him feel confident about whom he was. He could now live comfortably. His wallet, in the past often

A family celebration in Brighton. Antonio's mother-in-law is at left, the author's wife, Penny, is standing. The table was never large enough.

empty, now was fat with bills of large denominations, a measure of the pride he felt.

My earliest memories go back to when I was about 4 or 5 years old and our family lived on 8th street. We had moved there six months after I was born in September of 1944 (I was the child with whom my Mom was pregnant on the journey from New Mexico to Colorado.) I was the first one in the family to be born in Brighton and I was the first girl of the family. My mother walked to the hospital on Bridge Street from the family's two-room house on 9th street (about a half a mile). She had had so many boys she was not expecting a girl and was incredulous when the doctor announced, "It's a girl." She didn't have a girl's name chosen, but there was nurse in the delivery room and her name was Lucille. My mom thought that was a nice name and so that is what she named me.

As I grew up I longed for female companionship, but my mother had two more boys after me. Then at the age of 44 she had another girl, Catherine, but by that time I was 11 years old, the gap too big to really have the kind of relationship I wanted with a sister. We are close today and the 11 years between us seem like nothing.

Three of my older brothers were already gone from our home by the time I was in the first grade. I lament that I didn't get to grow up with them and didn't get to know them, as I would have liked.

When I was 6 or 7 years old we moved from the house on 8th Street to 822 South 4th. I was out playing in the huge yard when Mrs. Dunham, one of our new neighbors, came over and looked at me over her bifocals and asked, "Mexican are you?" That was the first time in my life I ever was asked that question. I ran in the house and told my mother about it and asked her if we were Mexican. She said no, "We are Spanish-Americans." She said we had never been to Mexico and we had no relatives in Mexico. She told me her ancestors had come to land now in the United States long before Mexico existed as a country. I never forgot Mrs. Dunham's question about my ethnicity but got the feeling she thought that was not a good thing to be. She commented on the fact that I could speak both English and Spanish.

I think my siblings who were born and lived in New Mexico could speak Spanish better than my siblings who were born after our family arrived in Brighton. I've always thought knowing two languages is like being able to enter two different worlds. We benefited greatly by being exposed to Spanish and English.

Coming from a large family has been a wonderful experience with positives and negatives. I miss sitting down to dinner with many siblings. I have many memories of the dinners I used to share with my big family. It seemed, though, that we never had enough food for the whole family.

Of Rollaway Beds and Second Hand Shoes

My grandfather, Enrique Perea, came to live with us when I was 16 years old. He was in his 90's. My father added on a room for him. Even though my mother had so many children and so many responsibilities, she agreed with her siblings that she would let Grandpa live with us.

Dad didn't always seem ok with the idea of his father-in-law living with us and he sometimes berated Grandpa in front of Mom and that would make her very sad. He didn't like Grandpa getting up early in the morning because that is when Dad had alone time with Mom before he went to work.

Before my father built Grandpa his own room, I sometimes would sleep on the sofa in our living room and Grandpa slept on a rollaway bed a few feet away from me. My brother Ray slept on the other sofa. I certainly never had my own bedroom like kids have today, because times were different then and my parents could not afford that. The house was small and my brothers shared beds, maybe three in a bed. At one time I slept on a rollaway bed in my parents' bedroom.

I have vivid memories of sleeping on a rollaway bed. At one time, my mom had me sleeping in her and Dad's bedroom because there was no other place for me to sleep. We knew nothing of having our own room as so many kids have today. Despite the hardships, those were fun times. We may not have had much as far as material things go, but we had a great family. We didn't know we were poor.

Growing up, there were always many people coming and going through the house. And no matter how few beds we had, when relatives visited us, somehow my parents would make a place for them to sleep. One night about 11 pm, after my parents had already gone to bed, we heard a tap, tap, and tap on the kitchen window. Tia Juanita, Dad's sister who lived in Wyoming, and her husband and family had driven to Brighton to visit us. We all got up to visit with them and Mom started cooking up a late dinner for them. Mom and Dad pulled out the rollaway beds and everyone had a place to sleep. It was not a big deal, not a problem, no one complained. We were just happy to see our relatives and they didn't have to call first before they showed up.

We didn't get to do much shopping, but I often went to the Segunda (second-hand store) with Mom and she bought us second-hand clothes and shoes. On one of our Segunda excursions I saw a little pair of black patent leather shoes and I asked Mom to buy them for me. They were only 75 cents, but in those days that was a lot of money for a pair of second-hand shoes. I begged Mom to get them for me and she relented. "Try them on," she said. I did and they were so tight I could hardly walk, but I told her they fit me just fine. She bought them and when I got home I asked Dad to cut a hole in the toe. He did and after that the shoes fit great. My big toe was sticking out of the front of the shoe, but did I care? No, I loved those little patent leather shoes.

Before Grandpa came to live with us, possibly when I was 9 or ten years old, Tia Ignacita Sandoval (Dad's oldest sister) and Grandmother Teodorita Sandoval moved to Colorado from New Mexico. They lived in some shacks on my Dad's property. I worried about them living there because they had no running water and the structures were at one time used as chicken coops. As I think back on how many hardships Tia Ignacita and Grandmother Sandoval suffered in those times, my heart breaks for them. Tia Ignacita never married even though she reportedly had many men ask for her hand. Being a single woman she always had to worry about making a living for herself and her adoptive daughter Priscilla and for Grandmother Sandoval. I remember she once got a job washing dishes at the "Stop-N-Eat" restaurant in Brighton. She had to walk home about a mile at 10:30 p.m. every night when the restaurant closed. She would sometimes bring us potato chips from the restaurant. Tia Ignacita and Grandmother Teodorita prayed the rosary and were very religious. Tia Ignacita eventually got a job as the cook and housekeeper for the priests at the Catholic parish in Greeley. Her life was better then and she lived in a little house near the church.

My parents and siblings often prayed the rosary together as a family. After dinner, we would all go into the living room and get on our knees and pray the rosary. Sometimes my brother (Eusebio) JR and I would get in trouble for laughing and horsing around while the family was trying to pray. My mother would reach over and pinch us both and that would make us laugh more.

Going to Mass before school and attending catechism class were a big part of my life when I was growing up. First Holy Communion and Confirmation ceremonies were something very special. I remember going to Church for the Stations of the Cross during Lent. My parents were deeply involved with the Church and my Dad used to take a truckload of altar boys up to the mountains for a picnic.

I attended Brighton Public Schools most of my life except when at the age of 14, my parents sent me to live with my oldest brother Moises in Dubuque, IA. I attended the Immaculate Conception Academy for one year and then decided I missed my Mother too much and went back to Brighton Public Schools. After graduating from Brighton High School I attended the College of Saint Teresa in Winona, MN, where my brother Arsenio was a professor. After that, at the age of 20 I married and moved to San Francisco for 10 years. During my first marriage, I went back to school and earned a bachelor's degree in journalism and technical writing. I divorced in 1982 and married Charles Branch, the dean of the School of Education at Metropolitan State College in 1983. Francheska, my daughter from my first marriage, is a school librarian in the Jefferson County Public Schools system.

Disciplinarian Dad

When I was a child I hated Dad because I thought he was so mean. He was a disciplinarian and often gave us a beating for something he saw as misbehaving. He disciplined me and my siblings the way his parents disciplined him and that meant physical beatings. If there is anything that I think marred my childhood and the wonderful family in which I grew up; it was Dads disciplinary tactics. By the time I had grown up he had mellowed out and he and I had a better relationship than we did when I was a kid. So probably all of my life I have had a love/hate relationship with my father. I have long forgiven him, however, for what I felt were injustices and transgressions on his part. I came to understand that he had tremendous responsibility in raising such a huge family of mostly boys. I am sure he felt inadequate when he couldn't find jobs to support his family. I can understand now many years later, how this contributed to Dad's short temper. Dad was impatient with us, but he was a good man who wanted the best for his family. I recall many jobs he had before he started his landscape business. At one time, I remember my mother saying he only made $49 a week. That was in the mid-1950s. All winter long, we had to charge the groceries that we bought at Friedman's Grocery store. Then when Dad got a job, we were able to pay off the grocery bill. Times were tough on the family, but Mother and Dad gave us so much more than money could ever buy. Mom especially was always happy and so optimistic. She always made us feel that we were capable of anything. "When there's a will, there's a way," she used to say. When I had a dilemma I didn't think I could solve my Mom would make me feel better. After telling her my tale of woe she would say, "Ok, Vamos a pensar." (Ok, let's think about it.) So we would go into the living room and sit down on the sofa and she would present possible scenarios for solving my problem. By the time we were done talking, I felt much better and could see things a lot more clearly.

A High School Experience

During the 60's when I was in high school I tried out for the cheerleading squad at Brighton High School. I wanted to be one of six cheerleaders that were chosen every year. When the votes came in I was the 6th cheerleader; I had made the cut, but one of the graduating cheerleaders said, "Lucy only has a few more votes that Ruth Ann, let's give it to Ruth Ann." Luckily a friend of mine, Linda Valdez, who also was a graduating cheerleader and was helping count the votes, opposed that idea. She said Lucy won, fair and square and we should give it to her. Linda was the only Latina on the squad when she was a cheerleader. Since then I've often wondered how many more of us have been cheated out of an opportunity because someone deemed us unworthy for no other reason than our ethnicity. Dad used to recite an Old Spanish proverb, "El pobre, aunque madruga, siempre llega tarde." (The poor man, though he rises early, always arrives late.) I've never forgotten that. The inside track is often very hard to jump on because one usually doesn't know about it.

Sign of the Times

Something that marked the sign of the times in the mid- to late-50's was exemplified in a lie told repeatedly about a young woman and her son. Shortly after we moved to South 4th Avenue a Hispanic family moved in across the street. They too had many children. One of their daughters had a little boy. Everyone knew he wasn't her brother. She and her family told everyone that the little boy's father had been in the military and had died fighting a war. In those times not many babies were born out of wedlock and birth control in pill form was nonexistent. Bertha's family said that she had been married when the little boy was born and we all just went along with that story even though we suspected otherwise. It was a sad commentary for everyone involved or associated with the lie, but the denial seemed necessary in those times. This situation has remained in my mind for all of these years. It is amazing how times have changed. Some high schools even have day care centers for students' babies. People no longer lie about their non-married pregnant teenage daughters.

On Being Female in an all male Family

Sometimes being the only female child in a large family of boys led me down a precipitous path. I had to compete with my brothers, yet I could not do everything they did. Sometimes my father would say that it didn't matter what I thought because I was a girl. Consequently, I've not always spoken up and given my opinion because in my mind's ear I can still hear Dad saying, "Tu no cuentas, tu eres mujer." (You don't count, you are a woman). He felt it was more important for the boys to get an education and a good job than it was for me. I think he thought I would just get married and have lots of children like he and Mom had. But unbeknownst to all, the times were changing. The day was coming when a large percentage of women would be going to college, not just to find husbands, but also to earn degrees and to compete in the workforce. Most women would no longer be having large families. And for the most part, stay-at-home moms would be a thing of the past. When I would ask my parents why my brothers could go to certain places or do certain things and I could not, they would say, "Because you are a girl and they are boys." My brothers teased me and punched me on the arm and snapped a towel on my butt. I screamed for Mom; and irritated by my screams, Dad would say, "Huye del peligro." (Run from the danger.) When my brother Tony was home from college he would protect me. "Be nice to your sister," he would say. "Don't hit your sister, boys don't hit girls." At any rate, I received my bumps and bruises, but I soon learned how to protect myself by being aggressive when I had to be or by getting my petty little revenge when I had the chance. I'll never forget blowing my nose on my brother's freshly ironed shirtsleeves. Looking back now on the odyssey of being Lucy, I wonder if my rollaway bed experience was symbolic of the feelings I had of having no place in an all male family. My parents didn't quite know what to do with me. They had never had a daughter before. They didn't know quite how to protect me or treat me, so they put me on a rollaway bed and sometimes they rolled me into their bedroom, sometimes into the living room and sometimes even into the basement. I didn't really have a permanent place to sleep. Where was my place? I didn't always know, and I didn't always know where my place was in the all male family. I sometimes felt like a lost little girl. I seemed to have survived it all, however. I did go to college like my brothers. I worked as a public relations professional for Metropolitan State College of

Denver and, for several years, for the University of Colorado at Denver. Growing up with so many brothers is quite a unique experience and I am glad it happened to me. I learned how to survive in a family made up of mostly males.

Hide the Tortillas

I can still remember the wonderful aroma of my mom's tortillas cooking on the stove. We were eating them faster than she could roll them out. Today one can buy tortillas in just about any grocery store, but when I was growing up only our Hispanic mothers made fresh tortillas every day. Our gringo friends didn't experience those delicious tortillas the way we did. In retrospect I pity them, for they sure missed out on the most wonderful tasting food I have ever had. One day after mom had made a huge stack of tortillas; she put them on the table and suddenly there was a knock at the door. Somebody yelled, "Hide those tortillas!" We wanted to hide them not for fear that they would all get eaten up, but because we felt a little embarrassment because the tortillas were a symbol of our ethnicity and in those times we just wanted to blend in. We wanted to enter the mainstream. We wanted to lose our uniqueness. If only we had known then that the popularity of the tortilla would set us free. Today eating tortillas is like eating wonder bread, bagels, croissants, dinner rolls or hotdog buns. No more need to hide the tortillas!

Tortillas by Long Distance

(Article by Moises Sandoval in El Grito del Sol, A Chicano Quarterly, April-June 1976)

Stomach knows no craving like a Chicano's longing for tortillas. Many a sad-faced soldier on foreign soil has longed not for his girl back home, but for tortillas. And today, as yesterday, many a shaky marriage is held together–believe it or not–by tortillas. For the tortilla is more than just bread, more even than the crust that makes many an inferior dish palatable. The tortilla is the Chicano's ultimate link with heritage, home, and Mother. Deep in his heart, every Chicano knows that no machine or other human hands can make tortillas like one's own Mother. And a wife who can even approximate Mother's prowess is worth her weight in tortillas!

For such a simple recipe–flour, lard, baking powder, salt and water–

the making of tortillas is high art. Many a wife has despaired of ever meeting her husband's standard. A good tortilla not only has taste and aroma, but also the strength to hold all the goodies one might want to wrap in it without being leathery. The tolerances in the process, however, are too fine for many women, and the result is either too brittle or hard to chew. If, like my wife, you're Irish instead of Chicana, the odds on coming up with a truly good tortilla are just too long. So, our marriage is beset with a series of recurrent tortilla crises which, like tropical malaria, ravage me every so often.

The last time this happened, I took the dough into my own hands, so to speak. First I dialed Mother two thousand miles away and asked her for an exact recipe. But part of the problem had been that Mother never measures ingredients. She takes a few handfuls of flour, a bit of salt, a little of this and a little of that, a splash of water, etc. It works fine for her, but it sure drives daughters-in-law up the wall. This time I left nothing to chance. I made Mother measure the ingredients exactly, give me stove and water temperatures, and the approximate cooking time. The results, while not quite as good as the tortillas that Mother makes, were tasty enough to make me file the recipe in my safety deposit box.

However, I cannot eat tortillas without feeling a trace of guilt. That's because my old civics teacher (in Brighton, CO.) preached regularly against tortilla eating. Being the only Chicano in class, and somewhat timid, I never questioned her on why tortilla eating was inconsistent with being a good American, a theme she emphasized daily. Finally, one of the students asked "Why?"

"Because tortillas are made with white flour," replied the teacher. "They're not as good for you as whole-wheat bread and we all know from our health classes that we should eat whole-wheat bread to have strong bodies. That's one reason why Mexicans are so short. They're always eating tortillas."

I thought long and hard about what Miss (Olive) Carr had said. Of course it was unthinkable to stop eating tortillas. But, I thought, if we made them with whole-wheat flour her objection would not hold. So I went home and told Mother she should make our tortillas with whole-wheat flour. Being a sweet and loving woman, Mother decided to try even though she was somewhat dubious about whether or not it would work. Soon she was turning out brown instead of white tortillas.

But tortillas made with whole-wheat flour just aren't the same.

They're bitter and hard to chew. No one in our family liked them. I tried to sway them on the basis of nutrition. But the meals became less and less cheerful as the days wore on. One day, while trying to chew a particularly leathery wheat tortilla, Father finally exploded: "Don't make any more whole-wheat tortillas. I don't care if they're better for you. I don't care what Miss Carr or anyone else thinks. From now on it is white flour tortillas!"

We never again saw another brown tortilla. And, Miss Carr notwithstanding, we ate them morning, noon, and night. Today, whenever work or vacation takes us home again, Mom greets us with a batch of freshly made tortillas which disappear in no time at all.

On these occasions, I think again of old Miss Carr, long since gone to her Anglo heaven, and I wonder what sad experience could have turned her so strongly against our tortillas, and why she found eating them so incompatible with being a good American. Were she living now, surely she would be shocked at the way the tortilla (much inferior to Mother's, of course) has wormed its way into supermarkets all the way across America. No doubt Miss Carr would have linked the tortilla's spreading popularity with the decline of patriotism and the weakening of the nation's moral fiber.

Ray Romero

(From a report by the author to the Alicia Patterson Foundation in 1977)

Ray Romero, (a cousin) who worked in the same fields as our family, lost his father, Juan Romero, at an early age and his widowed mother was left with the heavy task of bringing up seven children. Ray began working in the fields when he was four years old. Today, he is an assistant dean of students at Northern Colorado University in Greeley, Colo. His wife, Bella, who quit school at 15 to marry Ray, then only 18 years old, is now a kindergarten teacher in the Brighton school system, having finally received her college degree in her mid-30s. They have four children.

Ray worked in the fields until he was 14 although he admits that during the last two he found rolling dice much more profitable than picking peas and beans or topping onions. By the time he was in the fifth grade, he was working in the school cafeteria for 25 cents a week. During high school summer vacations he was a dishwasher, warehouseman and cannery worker. Married before he graduated from high school, he and Bella had to live with his mother for seven years before starting their own household. He was already a father when he was in college and it took him 5-1/2 years to get his first degree. Bella worked to help with finances but there were times when food was short. "Those were days of $5 a week for groceries," Ray said. "We ate corn tortillas for months at a time."

Cousin Ray Romero in 1977.

His first teaching job paid only $4,300 a year, but he stayed with it three years. Then he became a Head Start director and, after several years, an educational consultant, a job which took him to 45 states. In between, Ray said he "took time here and there" to pursue graduate studies. Going to Kent State University (in Ohio) for a master's degree meant leaving his family at home in Colorado, but he made the sacrifice. Then he went to the University of Illinois when he received a fellowship for studies toward a doctorate.

He also found time to get a certificate in administration at the University of Northern Colorado, where he became assistant dean of special services about 2-1/2 years ago. Though Ray was the only member of his family to complete college, none of his brothers or sisters remained in the fields. John, the eldest, has just retired at the age of 48 after 30 years of federal service–at an Army hospital beginning at age 14, as a paratrooper and as an employee at Rocky Mountain Arsenal. Dale tried the lettuce fields of Arizona before he gave up farm work and went into construction work. Manual quit school in the 9th grade, altered his birth certificate so he could get a job at Rocky Mountain Arsenal, served as a Green Beret in the Armed Forces and returned to the Arsenal, where he is about to complete 30 years of federal service. The remaining family members, three sisters, married men who do not work as farm laborers.

[The Romeros are children of cousin Pablita and Juan Romero. From Rociada, NM, they moved to Colorado about the same time we did and settled in Brighton.

Most of us had no trouble saying goodbye to Brighton, but Ray Romero decided to commute to Greeley rather than move away. He served on the Brighton Board of Education.]

CHAPTER THIRTEEN

THE ROOTS OF SUCCESS

The people of Terromote and surrounding communities succeeded because they had a quality described by the physicist Fred Alan Wolf in a book on quantum physics.[1] Wolf wrote that the quantum leap is the explosive leap that every particle in the material universe has to make or cease to exist. "In a figurative sense," he wrote, "it means to take a risk, to launch into unknown territory without any guide."

The people of the New Mexico highlands made that quantum leap not once but repeatedly, continuing to the present day. Everything was unknown territory for them—the work they did in urban society, the high schools and colleges they attended, the mainstream neighborhoods where they settled, and the multicultural marriages they entered into. But they didn't hesitate to seek new horizons, geographic, social, or economic.

They were able to do this because, as has been written about President Barack Obama, they were comfortable in their own skin. They knew who they were and were proud of their heritage. They did not feel they had to morph into Anglos in order to succeed. As these personal histories show, they saw themselves as successes, with skills, values and social structures to survive and advance. When they had faced injustice in the past they had fought against it. They had therefore a sense of history that what they now faced was not new, only a different environment. They were secure in their culture, and they never felt they were leaving it. They were taking it with them, whether they moved to Albuquerque or Denver.

Sometimes one hears of New Mexicans who do not take advantage of opportunities in other parts of the country because they do not want to leave the extended family and the community where they have always lived. The people in this book had no such fear because they were not going alone. When Amada and Eusebio Sandoval moved to Brighton, they already had a place to stay when they got there, the home of sister Quirina and brother-in-law Filadelfio. That is the process by which communities re-establish themselves. It begins with one intrepid pioneer who succeeds. Then other relatives follow and they benefit from the experience of those already there. Gradually, they recreate the essentials of their community. The Protestant theologian Justo Gonzalez once said that a culture has to be permeable or it dies. The culture of the people of the Sangre de Cristo foothills thrived because it was open to the cultures around it. We realized that Anglos, Asians and blacks had ideas worth adapting. Thus our culture gained new dimensions without disappearing. The Hispanic culture today in Brighton, CO, differs from the one in Tierra Monte. It has been modified by Anglos, the Mexican nationals and Asians. But it is still Hispanic and is perhaps more secure than ever. The Mexican novelist Carlos Fuentes wrote: "People and their cultures perish in isolation, but they are born or reborn in contact with other men and women, with men and women of another culture, another creed, another race."[2]

That sense of cultural security has been growing nationwide for more than half a century. Everywhere during and after World War II, Hispanics began to move ahead–the first in a family finishing high school or going to college, founding a little business, overcoming the barriers of mainstream society to becoming an apprentice in a building trade, gaining a new skill. Today Hispanics are in every field, including medicine, the law, business, education and even in the clergy and episcopacy, to be sure not as many as there should be but a great advance from a time when there were none. Roberto Lopez, a Los Angeles Times reporter who graduated from the most dysfunctional high school in the city in 1989, found that, within 10 years, the vast majority of his classmates had achieved the benefits of the middle class, including a 28 percent college graduation rate and high levels of marriage, children and home ownership.

After World War II, many benefited from new skills learned while in military service, the educational benefits offered by the G. I. Bill, hiring preferences for veterans applying for federal jobs, the example of immigrants from Latin America who, having been displaced by civil wars, would otherwise have had no need to abandon their homelands. The labor shortages during wartime had opened many jobs for Hispanics that in previous times had been reserved for Anglos.

However, the people of New Mexico, especially those in remote rural communities, appear to have had an advantage not shared by those who lived in states where they had always been a minority. They did not first have to overcome the debilitating effects of discrimination before they could move ahead. Isolation had protected them. Children had the time to develop, test ideas, dream, experiment, and find the limits of their imagination, all part of the process of maturing. Moreover, raising children was not as in today's society the lonely job of the nuclear family, sometimes that of a single parent. In these communities, it was everyone's job—beginning, of course, with the parents but extending to the grandparents, aunts, uncles, cousins, neighbors and the community at large.

In that society, written off as backward by outsiders, the children received the foundation for their success, their formation in the Latino civil society, as Dr. David Hayes-Bautista of the UCLA Medical School, identified it in his writings about Latinos in California: "The Latino civil society provides to young children their initial introduction to the world of right and wrong, the desirable and the undesirable, duty and dereliction.... their first notions of civic responsibility and their first hints of personal identity."[3] By the time they moved to other areas, the land, culture, faith and traditions had programmed them to succeed.

Moreover, they knew they had a homeland to which they could always return. For years, when we drove across the state line on visits home, we used to stop the car, get down and kiss the ground. That unbreakable identification remains, which is why many return to New Mexico after they retire in other states. It is why my brothers, sister-in-law and I still own part of the ranch developed by great Grandfather Estanislado Sandoval and Grandfather Octaviano Sandoval.

But a homeland, like culture, is not static. It is either growing or dying out. For Hispanics in the United States that homeland has been expanding from its base in the Southwest (and Latin America) to the great cities all across the country. Carlos Fuentes wrote that Los Angeles is now the second largest Spanish-speaking city in the world, smaller than Mexico City but larger than Madrid and Barcelona. "You can prosper in South Florida even if you speak only Spanish, as the population is predominantly Cuban. San Antonio, integrated by Mexicans, has been a bilingual city for 150 years."[4] He predicted that by mid-21st century, almost half the population of the United States would be Spanish-speaking. Already, in his view, a whole civilization with an Hispanic pulse has been created in the U.S. It is economic, political, and cultural, with its own literature, art, music and religious expression. The people of Terromote are but a microcosm of it.

Mainstream society, however, failed to notice the advance of Hispanics. Nearly four decades after that surge began, a prestigious history published in 1987 on the Catholic parish in the United States had a chapter by a West Coast historian who had this to say about Hispanics:

"Being out of touch with the American church, the Mexican American has found other elements of American culture difficult to accept. The Mexican American sense of alienation has been increased by his or her inability to relate to the American work ethic. Nor was the ambition to succeed highly prized. Satisfaction was found in one's family and friends. To outsiders this was often interpreted as sloth. The lack of initiative made many Anglos assume that the Mexican American was best suited for menial labor. Neither did the Mexican family place much emphasis on formal education."[5]

Several years after the book was published, the author of that chapter and I were on a committee at the University of Notre Dame advising the Cushwa Institute for the Study of American Catholicism on the design of a new history of the Hispanic Church. He was very angry that I had used the above citation in demonstrating the stereotypes we have had to overcome. But if he had recognized his mistake, many in the dominant culture continue to see Hispanics as a minus rather than a plus.

Public opinion clings to the view that Hispanics are a dysfunctional culture with the potential of lowering the country's standard of living. That is at the base of the virulent opposition to undocumented immigrants. Lawrence Downes of the New York Times writes that bigots pour all their loathing of Spanish-speaking people into the word illegal, "call them congenital criminals, lepers, thieves, unclean." To counter it, Hispanics need a literature of success, to which this work contributes.

We have come a long way, but we are not there yet!

----

[1]Fred Alan Wolf, *Taking the Quantum Leap: The New Physics for Non-Scientists* (San Francisco: Harper and Row, 1981) p. 1.
[2]Carlos Fuentes, *The Buried Mirror: Reflections on Spain and the New World* (New York: Houghton Mifflin Co., 1992) p. 353.
[3]David E. Hayes-Bautista, *La Nueva California: Latinos in the Golden State* (Berkeley: University of California Press, 2004) Introduction.
[4]Carlos Fuentes, Op. Cit., p. 343.
[5]Jeffrey M. Burns, "Building the Best: History of Catholic Parish Life in the Pacific States," in Jay P. Dolan, *The American Catholic Parish: A History from 1850 to the Present* (New York: Paulist Press, 1987) Vol. II, p. 87.

CHAPTER FOURTEEN

EPILOGUE

Terromote, now Tierra Monte, has gone through several stages of habitation. The first, of course, was that of the original settlers. When they left during and after the Great Depression and World War II, only a few families remained, among them Herman Sandoval, Patrociño Gomez, and one or more Quintana families. Then in the 1960s, hippies discovered the abandoned houses and moved in before the whirlwind took them to God knows where.

Inevitably, in the third stage, the Anglos came–from Dallas, Amarillo and other places in Texas; from Los Alamos, Santa Fe and Albuquerque in New Mexico, even from Florida. Once in a while, one of them, with typical hubris, says they have to educate us. They bid up the price of land to where an acre purchased by Enrique Perea for $2 now goes for as much as $5,000.

At the same time, some of Herman Sandoval's sons and daughters built homes on land he gave them. Then other Hispanics without roots in Terromote began to buy a few acres here and there for a home. For the first time in Terromote's history there are almost enough homes for a village on lots sold by Herman Sandoval.

In the fourth stage, some of those who were born there and went away have come back, like Celestino Aragon and Arsenio Sandoval. I also have a home there, about half a mile from the house where I was born on Grandpa Octaviano's ranch, but do not yet live there full-time. Many others come to visit or vacation here. Some say this is where their ashes should be scattered when their earthly journey ends.

Back in 1960 when Aunt Ignacita, having inherited half of Grandpa Octaviano's ranch, was going to sell it to a Texan, I proposed to her: "I can organize my brothers to buy it; sell it to us." We bought her 555 acres and later added 24 purchased from Cousin Connie Gregory, daughter of Aunt Carolina Padilla, which we needed for access.

Here the great grandchildren and of Enrique Perea and Octaviano Sandoval come from Boston, Houston, Phoenix, Tampa, Oak Ridge (TN), Denver, Hartford and Los Angeles to listen to the whisper of the breeze through the Ponderosas, photograph the abundant wildflowers, pick some of the wild oregano and medicinal herbs, hike through the valleys and up hills as high as 8,500 feet above sea level, take in the breath-taking vistas, or simply bask in the sun. No need to do without electricity, inside water and plumbing, telephone, satellite television and the Internet. We have them all.

We welcome our children and grandchildren along with the bluebirds in the spring, the hummingbirds in the summer, the blue jays and the elk in the fall. Rancho Carmel, named for a brother who died too soon, is theirs to enjoy. They are all stockholders in The Sandoval Corporation, dedicated to preserve this land for the enjoyment of future generations of the family. As they walk this land, we want them to establish a strong link with their ancestors, their culture and their history. If they can do that, they can make it anywhere!

One of those who returned

(A column by Moises Sandoval published by the Catholic News Service in 2006)

I go to church at Upper Rociada because of Antonia Apodaca," says Nurse Amy Chavez, of Tierra Monte, NM. She drives 10 miles for

Antonia Apodaca, of Rociada.

the joy of hearing the hymns played on the accordion by Apodaca, a slender and petite 82-year-old who has played in the White House for the elder George Bush, for governors of New Mexico and for countless audiences, the powerful and the humble. She performed at the Festival of American Folk Art at the Smithsonian Institute and the National Museum of American History, both in Washington, D. C. Recipient of many honors, she has many engagements but still finds time to play in humble churches like the chapel in Rociada.

Yet it is difficult to say what is more impressive, the music or the musician. "Antonia is a stunningly energetic and dynamic musician and human being," wrote admirer David Romvedt. "For her there is no separation between music and life. When she performs, it is as if we are all friends sitting around the living room. There is a great compassion and love in Antonia that shines through when she performs and when she is helping another person learn about her music and life."

If her music puts us in touch with the infinite love of God, she also teaches us to live life fully, not letting age limit our possibilities. She had just performed in Taos, Española, Albuquerque and Clayton. Now she was going play at the Santuario de Chimayo, a favorite shrine for pilgrims in New Mexico. "My daughter-in-law needs a liver transplant and I hope it helps to raise funds," she said. From there she was going to play for a wedding. "You have to jump around to stay alive," she told me, as she observed dancers at a birthday party. Alone or with other musicians, she gives concerts for all age groups, teaches Spanish colonial dances and songs, and gives workshops on playing the accordion and the guitar and on songwriting.

Antonia learned how to play the accordion at the age of six from her mother, Rafaelita Suazo Martínez. She had learned it from her husband, José Damacio Martínez. In turn she had taught him how to play the guitar, which she had learned from her father, Abran Suazo. Music runs deep in Antonia's family. The family had a small band and Antonia played and sang in it. At 13, she won an accordion contest in Santa Fe, competing against adults. A few years later, Max Apodaca joined the band, and he and Antonia fell in love. They were married in 1943.

Like many poor Hispanics, the Apodacas followed the migrant trail planting, cultivating and harvesting crops. Eventually, they settled in Riverton, WY., where he worked as a uranium miner. They raised their five children there and continued playing music together. Returning to Rociada in 1979, they settled in a house they had built in the early 1940s. When he died, in 1987, Antonia stopped playing and singing, devastated by her loss. Two friends helped her to start again and she has not stopped. She said she especially loves the *rancheras*, songs telling of the struggle of people who had to abandon their land in New Mexico and seek a living elsewhere.

People constantly drop by to visit Antonia, some of them neighbors and some from far-away places. She still lives in the house she and her husband built 60 years ago, without running water and inside plumbing. The visitors marvel at her vitality, undimmed by age and struggle. She is a cultural icon throughout New Mexico and beyond.

Teddy Aragon and William Suazo wedding; ring bearer is Eusebio Sandoval Jr.; flower girl is Lucy Sandoval.

Aunt Elis Martinez lived to age 93 and died in 2008.

Gregory Sandoval, son of Eusebio Jr. and Sally Sandoval

Clan of George and Dulcinea Olivas and Conrado and Juanita Aragon, in Colorado.

Agustina and Mary Ann Perea, of Manuelitas, the keepers of the memories in the Perea family.

Clockwise from left, Aunt Timotea, Cleo Perea, Josie Aragon and Marcella Perea.

THE PEOPLE OF TERROMOTE
(A partial directory)

Josefita and Enrique Perea
  Amada, homemaker
  Jose Dolores, deputy sheriff-
    cook
  Juan, miner
  Melecio, police chief-sheriff
  Pedro, shepherd-railroad
    laborer
  Quirina, homemaker
**Teodorita and Octaviano
  Sandoval**
  Alfonso, railroad laborer
  Benjamin, driver-body guard
  Carolina, homemaker
  Dulcinea, homemaker
  Elis, homemaker
  Eusebio, farmer-landscaper
  Herman, farmer
  Ignacita, parish housekeeper
  Juanita, homemaker
  Octaviano Jr., railroad worker
  Pablita, homemaker
Amada and Eusebio Sandoval
  Antonio, chemist-deacon
  Arsenio, professor-teacher
  Carmel, professor-businessman
  Catherine, certified public
    accountant
  Elivinio, dentist
  Eusebio Jr., professor
  Frank, welder
  Lucy, university public relations
  Moises, journalist-editor
  Raymond, teacher
Dora and Alfonso Sandoval
  Alfonso, artist
  Charlie, restaurant owner
  Ernesto, car salesman
  Irene, social worker
  John, service station owner
  Julian, antique car mechanic
  Maria Katie, social worker
  Paul, contract carrier-cook
  Rafael, restaurant worker
  Ramon, carpenter

  Rita, artist-business owner
  Teresa, cafeteria supervisor
Simona and Herman Sandoval
  Anna, teacher's aide
  Andrew, rancher
  Mario, teacher
  Mary Ann, homemaker
  Elizabeth, office worker
  Jimmy,
  Herman,
  Eva, waitress
Pablita and Sam Alle
  Anthony Raymond, professor-
    realtor
  David, professional soldier
  Emma, homemaker
  Sara, beauty shop owner
  Virginia, homemaker
Juanita and Conrado Aragon
  Ben
  Celestino, upholsterer
  Ernie, welder
  Fabiola
  Josephine, nun-teacher
  Leo, service station owner-
    upholsterer
  Mary Jane
  Teodorita
Julia and José Dolores Perea
  Barbara, schools superintendent,
    state legislator
  Consuelo, cook
  Mary, homemaker
  Mickey, homemaker
Esther and John Perea
  Patrick, locomotive engineer
  Matthew, locomotive engineer
  Michael Angelo, security guard
Josie and Joe Montoya
  Danny, county employee
  Gerald, truck driver
  Gilbert, computer technician
  Mary Lou, beauty salon owner
  Philip, U.S. Postal Service
  Shirley, teacher

Penelope and Moises Sandoval
James, corporate finance manager
Mary, Ph.D., mathematics
 professor
Meg, journalist-print production
 manager
Michael, electrician
Rose, business owner
Martha and Anthony R. Alle
Martha Rose, massage therapist
Michael, mechanical engineer
Paula, nurse-realtor
Maud and Antonio Sandoval
Amada, director, women's center
Carlos, lawyer
Eusebio, teacher
Stella and José Perea
Anna, manufacturing equipment
 technician
Cynthia, pharmacist
Deborah, systems engineer
Jimmy, carpentry-maintenance
Lorraine, bilingual educational
 diagnostician
Richard, president of Landmark
 Investment Co., Inc.
Lucille and Elivinio Sandoval
Christina: Public health
David, pilot
Debbie, MD: anesthesiologist
Frances, MD: psychiatrist
John, MD: anesthesiologist
Judy, homemaker
Patrick, graphic artist
Paul, MD: anesthesiology
Chun Hi and Arsenio Sandoval
Maria, judicial assistant
Patricia, teacher
Ruth, social worker
Steve, nuclear safety officer
Neva and Carmel Sandoval
Elena, Ph.D. in education
Lynda, novelist-writer-teacher
Loretta, physical therapist
Lucy and Charlie Branch
Francheska, school librarian

Josephine and Sebastian Jacquez
Yvette, marketing business owner
Sally and Raymond Sandoval
Ray Jr., chemist
Eleanor and Octaviano Sandoval Jr.
Ed, commercial photographer
Lisabet, collections agency
 worker
Tony, railroad worker
Irene, chef
Tillie and Melecio Perea
John, policeman-magistrate judge
Melecio, civil service
Eddie, state employee
Mary Jean, state employee
Rose Marie, state employee
Rose Marie Anne, state employee
Michael, state employee
Frances, corporation employee
Teddy and William Suazo
Harold, sales manager
Danny, store manager
Chris, Ph.D., instrumental music
 director, Madrid, Spain
Susan, beautician
Mary, computer technician

INDEX

www.ingramcontent.com/pod-product-compliance
Lightning Source LLC
Chambersburg PA
CBHW072144270326
41931CB00010B/1877